RESEARCHING SECOND LANGUAGE CLASSROOMS

ESL & Applied Linguistics Professional Series
Eli Hinkel, Series Editor

RESEARCHING SECOND LANGUAGE CLASSROOMS

Sandra Lee McKay

LEA LAWRENCE ERLBAUM ASSOCIATES, PUBLISHERS
2006   Mahwah, New Jersey   London

Lawrence Erlbaum Associates, Inc., Publishers
10 Industrial Avenue
Mahwah, New Jersey 07430
www.erlbaum.com

Cover design by Kathryn Houghtaling Lacey

Library of Congress Cataloging-in-Publication Data

McKay, Sandra.
    Researching second language classrooms / Sandra Lee McKay.
        p.   cm. — (ESL & applied linguistics professional series)
    Includes bibliographical references and index.
    ISBN 0-8058-5340-5 (pbk. : alk. paper)
    1. Language and languages—Study and teaching—Research—Methodology.   2. Second
language acquisition—Research—Methodology.   I. Title.   II. ESL and applied linguistics
professional series.

P53.755.M35   2006
407′.2—dc22   2005051011
                                                                                           CIP

Printed in the United States of America
10 9 8 7 6 5 4 3 2 1

Contents

Preface

Dawkins (2003), a professor of science at Oxford University, wrote the following to his ten-year-old daughter as he tried to explain to her the basis for scientific inquiry and research.

Dear Juliet,

Now that you are ten, I want to write to you about something that is important to me. Have you ever wondered how we know the things we know? How do we know, for instance, that the stars, which look like tiny pinpricks in the sky, are really huge balls of fire like the Sun and very far away? And how do we know that the Earth is a smaller ball whirling round one of those stars, the Sun?

The answer to these questions is "evidence." (p. 242)

This book is all about gathering evidence to answer questions about L2 teaching and learning. Whereas research methods differ in the kind of evidence they gather, all L2 classroom research involves the formulating of questions, as well as the gathering and analysis of evidence or data to answer these questions.

This text introduces research methods that can be used to answer questions regarding L2 teaching and learning, such as the following.

What beliefs do teachers have about the teaching of grammar?

What are students' attitudes toward the use of group work in L2 classes?

What reading strategies are used by proficient L2 readers?

How authentic is the language presented in L2 textbooks?

What social assumptions inform the content of L2 textbooks?

Becoming familiar with classroom-based research methods has two major benefits:

- first, it enables teachers to do research in their own classrooms; and
- second, it provides a basis for assessing the findings of existing research.

This book is addressed to novice researchers, whether they be graduate students, teachers, or administrators, who want to become familiar with methods commonly used in L2 classroom research.

This book is based on several assumptions regarding L2 classroom research.

- First, all researchers should begin the research process by clarifying their own beliefs about L2 teaching and learning and specifying the theories and assumptions that inform their study. Some researchers, for example, believe that cognitive and motivational factors are primary factors in language learning; others view social and cultural factors as more important. Some believe aspects of L2 teaching and learning can be isolated for analysis whereas others stress the need to view the process holistically. Because these beliefs will influence the questions that researchers ask, researchers should clarify for their readers their beliefs and assumptions.

- Second, research methods need to be judged in relation to the question asked. If, for example, a researcher wants to find out more about how L2 learners process written texts, then the method must be one that can provide insight into cognitive processes. On the other hand, if a researcher wants to look at interaction patterns in student group work, then the method must be one that examines oral discourse patterns. By focusing on a variety of methods, this book will demonstrate how all methods have their strengths and limitations. What researchers need to do is select the most appropriate method for answering the questions they ask and apply this method with rigor and integrity.

- Third, those involved in the research process need to be protected and benefitted. When researchers ask teachers and learners to participate in their research, they need to make certain that the participants are fully aware of the risks and benefits that can arise from taking part in the project. Because learners are typically in positions of less power, it is essential that they have every opportunity to decline participation with no negative consequences. In addition, the identity of the participants needs to be fully protected. Finally, it is important that those who participate in a research project gain some benefit, particularly in increasing their own understanding of L2 teaching and learning.

• Fourth, research is a rigorous process that involves specifying a research question, selecting a method that can best answer this question, gathering relevant data, and carefully analyzing this data. The process, although informed by reflection, must go beyond this. Although there is a need for reflection in the teaching process, it is a mistake to equate reflection with research. Rather reflection can provide the basis for research.

• Finally, those involved in L2 teaching and learning on a daily basis are in ideal positions to undertake classroom research. They are the ones who have a vested interest in better understanding L2 teaching and learning; they are aware of many of the classroom-based questions that need to be answered; and they have access to L2 classrooms. What they need is an understanding of the research process, as well as time and support to undertake research.

OVERVIEW

The book begins with a general introduction to major research purposes and research types as they relate to classroom research. A distinction is made between quantitative and qualitative research in terms of the role of the researcher, assumptions about reality, research questions, typical data gathered, data analysis, and research reports. The chapter also discusses the formulating of research questions and research designs. It ends with a discussion of ethical research.

In chapter 2, *Researching Teachers and Learners*, research methods that can be used to examine teachers' and learners' attitudes and behavior are introduced. The chapter opens with an introduction to *action research*, a method designed to address classroom problems through intervention. Next, *survey research* and the writing and analysis of survey questions are discussed. The chapter then introduces various types of *interviews* and makes suggestions for conducting interviews and analyzing the data that are gathered. The next section of the chapter deals with one of the few available methods for accessing students' cognitive processes, namely *verbal reports*. This is followed by an examination of how *diary studies* can be used to provide insight into the attitudes and beliefs of language teachers and learners. The chapter ends with an introduction to two qualitative research methods commonly used to holistically study L2 teachers and learners, namely, *case studies* and *ethnographies*.

Chapter 3, *Researching Classroom Discourse*, deals with methods that can be used to study the oral and written discourse of classrooms. Two methods for examining the oral exchanges of a classroom are examined—*interaction analysis* and *discourse analysis*. The second section of the chapter focuses on how *text analysis* can be used to study student texts, teachers' written feedback, and L2 teaching materials. The chapter also includes a discussion of how corpora can be used to study written classroom discourse. In closing, the chapter deals with ways to examine the social and political assumptions underlying the choice and presentation of content in L2 teaching materials.

The book ends with a chapter on writing research papers, with attention to both thesis writing and journal articles. The chapter begins by discussing guidelines for writing a thesis and journal article. Next, the chapter highlights the importance of using the introduction to clearly establish the purpose of a research project and the significance of the study. Then various ways of organizing a literature review are introduced. In discussing the writing of the methodology section, great emphasis is placed on the need to describe every aspect of the methodology in full detail. Recommendations are also made for displaying the results of data analysis. Finally, suggestions are made for writing conclusions.

Throughout the book, each chapter ends with suggestions for further reading. The list provides readers with references to particular areas of research they may want to investigate in greater depth. Within each chapter there are activities that help readers apply the methods described in the chapter, often by analyzing research data.

ACKNOWLEDGMENTS

I wish to thank several individuals for helping me with this project. First, my thanks go to Eli Hinkel and Naomi Silverman for encouraging me to write a book on L2 research methods. I would also like to thank Christine Goh, Anne Lazaraton, and Patricia Porter for their constructive suggestions on earlier drafts of the book, as well as my graduate students for their insightful questions in my research seminar. Finally, and most importantly, I thank my husband and family for their understanding and support.

—*Sandra Lee McKay*

Chapter 1

Classroom Research

This chapter explores the following questions:

- What are major types of research and how do they differ?
- What are the characteristics of sound research questions and designs?
- What ethical standards should researchers adhere to?

Before turning to these questions, let us consider the benefits of doing research. For teachers, a primary reason for doing research is to become more effective teachers. Research contributes to more effective teaching, not by offering definitive answers to pedagogical questions, but rather by providing new insights into the teaching and learning process. As Johnson (1992) puts it,

> The importance of research is not so much that it supplies definitive answers to questions such as "What is the best way to learn a language?" or "Which is the most effective method of L2 teaching?" It does not. Rather, research can help us gain a richer understanding of the many interrelated factors involved in learning. It can help us see how the ways we organize learning environments can promote or inhibit growth. (p. 5)

For some, action research is viewed as one of the most effective research methods for producing sound L2 teaching practices. This is because action research, by definition, involves a systematic inquiry into the issues and problems that teachers face with the goal of improving pedagogical practices. We examine the assumptions and approaches used in action research in chapter 2. However, this is not the only method that can be used to produce more effective L2 teaching and learning. All of the methods introduced in the book can be used to answer questions that directly involve decisions about pedagogical practices, thus contributing to the improvement of L2 teaching and learning.

A second reason for teachers to undertake classroom research is to better evaluate existing research. Once individuals become involved in the research process, they gain experience in forming research questions and selecting the methods that best answer these questions. They understand the challenges of analyzing data and drawing conclusions. They also become sensitive to the many practical problems that exist in doing research such as gaining access to classrooms, getting permission from participants, and having participants drop out of research projects. With this background, teachers can become more critical readers of existing research, carefully examining the conclusions of a study in light of the context and methods used.

In spite of these benefits, there are a variety of reasons why teachers may be hesitant or unable to undertake research. For one thing many teachers have not been trained to undertake research. Often teacher education programs focus primarily on how to teach, examining how to specify learning objectives, design lessons, and assess learning. Little or no attention is given to training teachers to rigorously investigate L2 classrooms. Hopefully reading this text will help alleviate this problem. Another factor that often discourages teachers from doing research are very practical issues such as heavy teaching loads or lack of support from administrators. Many of the methods suggested in this text can be used by teachers in their own classes, thereby reducing the additional time and administrative support needed to undertake research in other contexts. As a way of illustrating the various research designs that are possible, we turn now to an examination of the various meanings and purposes that research can have.

* * *

Exploring the Ideas, 1.1

In order to address some of the obstacles you face in doing research, begin by identifying a specific area of research you are interested in researching. Describe in as much detail as possible what you would like to investigate and in what context you would undertake this study. Then list the personal and professional obstacles you face in undertaking this research. Finally, consider how you might overcome these obstacles. If you can, share your findings with other teachers or classmates.

* * *

Exploring the Ideas, 1.2

In a journal entry, list your responses to the following questions. Then share your ideas with other teachers or classmates.

- In your view, what constitutes research? Is an L2 teacher who reflects on his or her teaching behavior in the classroom in order to solve a classroom problem involved in research? Why or why not?
- In general what do you see as the purpose of research in the area of L2 teaching and learning? Should research in this field have specific classroom applications?
- Do you think research is valuable in helping teachers teach more effectively? If so, list specific studies that have influenced your approach to teaching? If not, why do you think research is not relevant to the classroom?
- What are some issues you believe cannot be "researched" yet are clearly central to the teaching of English?

* * *

TYPES OF RESEARCH

Problems of Defining Research

There are several reasons why it is difficult to define research. The most significant reason is because research is multifaceted, differing in theoretical frameworks, goals, methods, and data sources. Another factor that contributes to the lack of a comprehensive definition of research is that the term often has unpleasant connotations, which lead some to avoid using the term altogether. Often in the field of L2 teaching and learning there are discussions of being a reflective teacher rather than arguments for teachers becoming researchers. Many graduate students share this negative attitude toward research. Brown and Rodgers (2002), for example, found that their graduate students listed words like *endless, painful, boring,* and *time consuming* when asked to free associate with the term.

In considering specifically what is meant by classroom research, Allwright and Bailey (1991) maintain that classroom research is a cover term for "a whole range of research studies on classroom language learning and teaching. The obvious unifying factor is that the emphasis is solidly on trying to understand what goes on in the classroom setting" (p. 2). For Nunan (1992) research must contain three essential elements: "(1) a question, problem or hypothesis, (2) data, (3) analysis and interpretation of data" (p.

3). Although these definitions provide a starting point for defining class-room research, what is needed to supplement these definitions is a more robust view of the types of inquiry that can be undertaken, the kinds of questions that can be asked, and the methods of data collection and analysis that can be used.

To provide a more comprehensive view of research we examine research from the perspective of what Richards (2003) terms

- *a paradigm* or "a set of basic beliefs" regarding research;
- *a tradition* or an "approach to research covering generally recognized territory and employing a generally accepted set of research methods;" and
- *a method* or "a means of gathering, analyzing and interpreting data using generally recognized procedures" (p. 12).

In what follows, we discuss the paradigm of basic and applied research, the major research traditions of qualitative and quantitative research, and end by describing some typical methods employed in L2 classroom research.

Research Paradigms: Basic Versus Applied Research

One of the most central distinctions made in discussing research is the difference between *basic* and *applied research.* The purpose of *basic research* is to acquire knowledge for the sake of knowledge. Its main goal is to contribute to a fuller understanding of the world. Often basic research is undertaken in disciplines like biology, physics, astronomy, and geology and is used by researchers who want to verify theories of their discipline. Cosmologists, for example, may be concerned about testing theories about the origin of the universe. Physicists may be concerned about verifying the qualities of molecules. But basic research is also a tradition in SLA. Research that seeks to verify such things as the order that learners acquire grammatical rules or the importance of input in language learning are examples of basic research in the field of SLA.

Applied research deals with human and societal problems in the hopes of finding solutions to real-world problems. A great deal of research in the field of TESOL is, of course, applied research. Second language educators, for example, have investigated why some students are reluctant to contribute to class discussions, what is the most effective type of feedback on student essays, and what is the most productive number of vocabulary items to introduce at one time. Applied research is more limited in its questions and conclusions. It does not attempt to define a theory of language learning that accounts for all language learners; rather it sets forth findings that apply to a particular time, place, and context.

There are two major sources of data that both basic and applied researchers can gather while conducting research. These are known as secondary and primary data. In using *secondary data*, researchers examine what others have discovered about a particular topic. For example, if teachers want to know about the advantages and disadvantages of using peer review in a writing class, they can investigate what others have written on the topic. As McDonough and McDonough (1997) point out, when secondary data is used, "the outcome of the research is the establishment, publicizing, or utilization of something that somebody—not the researcher or the person commissioning it—already knows" (p. 37).

One example of a study using secondary data is Silva (1993). In this study Silva summarized the findings of 72 empirical research studies that compared L1 and L2 writers with regard to their composing processes and the features of their written texts. He then discussed what these findings suggest in general for designing an effective L2 writing program. Studies such as these are termed *literature reviews*.

Typically, the reporting of all research projects begins with a literature review. One may well ask what the benefits are of beginning a research project by reviewing and summarizing the existing literature on a topic. By starting this way, researchers gain insight into what is already known about a particular topic and what still needs to be discovered. In other words, researchers avoid the problem of reinventing the wheel by examining issues that have already been investigated. Rather the researcher can contribute to knowledge in a field by exploring something that has not been adequately examined. In this way the research findings contribute to a real gap in knowledge about L2 teaching and learning.

In using *primary data*, researchers gather original data to answer a particular research question. As McDonough and McDonough (1997) note, when researchers gather first-hand data, "the outcome is knowledge nobody had before" (p. 37). Shortly we discuss various types of primary data that researchers can use to answer a research question. First, we distinguish two central research traditions and discuss the types of primary data that are typically used in each.

Research Traditions: Qualitative Versus Quantitative Research

One of the major distinctions made in discussing primary research is the difference between *quantitative* and *qualitative research*. In order to distinguish these two traditions, it is helpful to examine the differences in the types of research questions that are posed in these two traditions, as well the typical data that are used and how they are analyzed.

In quantitative research, a researcher typically begins with a research question or hypothesis that is quite specific. Chen and Graves (1995), for example, wanted to find out which type of reading preparation was most effective in increasing reading comprehension. In order to do this, they provided 243 non-English majors at a Taiwan university with different types of reading preparation. One group was introduced to a reading text by receiving background information about some of the content in the reading text. A second group was given a preview of what the text was about. Another group received both types of introduction and a fourth group received no preparation for the reading. Among their research questions were the following:

1. Did students who received the background knowledge or the previewing treatment comprehend better than those who did not receive these treatments?
2. Did students who received a combined treatment that included both background knowledge and previewing comprehend better than those who received only one treatment?
3. Were any of the treatments superior to the other? (p. 667)

Several aspects of this study make it a quantitative research project. First, the researchers assumed that reality could be broken down and investigated. In the study, Chen and Graves assumed that reading text preparation and reading comprehension could be isolated so that the relationship between them could be studied. In addition, attempts were made to minimize other variables such as the difficulty of the reading passage and the students' level of language proficiency, which might also affect reading comprehension. Chen and Graves also described their methodology before they undertook the study, specifying what would be done in each type of introductory session for the reading text, how long students would have to read the text, and how their comprehension would be assessed. The study involved a relatively large sample of students and the findings were reported with statistical analysis. Finally, the study was undertaken within a short time span. Table 1.1 summarizes some of the central features of quantitative research, all of which are evident in the Chen and Graves (1995) study.

Qualitative research, on the other hand, typically starts with the assumption that classroom learning must be studied holistically, taking into account a variety of factors in a specific classroom. One example of a qualitative research study is Willett (1995). In this study, Willett undertook a 4-year study of an international community of graduate students and their fami-

TABLE 1.1
Features of Quantitative and Qualitative Research

	Quantitative Research	*Qualitative Research*
Assumptions about reality	Reality is single; it can be broken down and parts studied.	Reality is multiple; it can only be studied holistically.
Role of researcher	The researcher and object of inquiry are separate; hence one can look at reality objectively. The researcher's role is to observe and measure. The researcher exerts control over the variables.	The researcher and what is researched are interdependent. The researcher's role is to become part of what is being studied. The researcher does not intervene.
Purpose of research	The purpose is to generalize, to predict, and to posit causal relationships.	The purpose is to contextualize and to interpret.
Research questions	The research question is arrived at deductively. The researcher starts with a hypothesis.	The research question is arrived at inductively. The researcher observes and formulates questions.
Research design	The researcher has a hypothesis and set methodology. The object is to summarize data in numerical indices.	The research design evolves over time. Once the data is gathered, the researcher looks for patterns.
Length of study	The study can involve a fairly short time commitment.	The study can involve a very long time commitment.
Typical data	There is a large, random sample. Numerical indices involving tests or responses to surveys are often used.	There is a purposeful, limited number of participants. Field notes, interviews, and written documents can all be used.
Data analysis	There is statistical analysis.	There is an interpretive analysis of the data and categorization of the data.
Research report	Technical language is used.	Descriptive language is used.

lies. In one phase of the study, Willett decided to observe a small group of L2 children who were enrolled in a mainstream first-grade classroom. Her general purpose was to study L2 socialization in a mainstream classroom. In order to do this, she decided to focus on specific classroom routines, one of which was a phonics recitation in which the teacher would elicit words from students that began with a particular target sound. With this general goal, she specified three general research questions:

1. What was the nature (linguistically and socially) of the recurring events selected for focus?
2. How did the ESL children participate in these events designed for native speakers?
3. How did their participation change over time as their competence grew? (p. 479)

In order to answer these questions she gathered a variety of data including classroom observations as a teacher's aide, detailed field notes, systematic audiotapes of three target first-graders with limited English proficiency, and documents from the classroom such as test results and school records. She also conducted extensive interviews with the parents and teacher of these children. Finally, she observed and took notes on the general academic life of the classroom, as well as life in the school and community. Having gathered this data, she consistently reviewed the data to discover recurring patterns regarding how the children were socialized into the specific learning patterns of the first-grade classroom, looking specifically at how their participation in the class changed as the children acquired more English language proficiency. Her findings were reported in descriptive language in which such things as classroom routines, the character of the target children, and their interactions were carefully detailed. What emerged was a description of the typical learning routines of this specific classroom and how the children learned from both the adults and friends with whom they interacted. No attempt was made to generalize these findings beyond the local context.

A variety of factors in this study exemplify aspects of qualitative research. First, Willett made no attempt to intervene in the typical activities of a classroom. The goal was not to posit a causal relationship, as was done in Chen and Graves' (1995) study. Rather Willett attempted to interpret what she observed happening in a particular context. Unlike typical quantitative research projects, which is deductive and designed to test hypotheses, qualitative research is inductive, using the data gathered to arrive at general conclusions rather than making hypotheses during the initial phrase of the study. In addition, unlike quantitative research, qualitative research generally involves a limited number of participants and in the case of ethnographic research, like Willett's study, can require a long time commitment, sometimes up to several years. The analysis of data generally entails arriving at original categories to summarize the data that was gathered. Depending on the method used, data can include field notes, interviews, conversations, verbal protocols, surveys, and written texts. Unlike a quantitative study, the findings are not reported using statistical procedures but rather rely on rich descriptions of typical scenes that were observed. Because of this, the language is descriptive rather than abstract. Table 1.1 summarizes general features of qualitative research, all of which are evident in the Willett study.

As is obvious there are significant differences between these two research traditions. However, each tradition can offer rich insights into the process of teaching and learning a second language. Which one to employ depends on a variety of factors: the research question that is being addressed, the preferences of the researcher, and the constraints that exist in undertaking the research. In this book we describe methods that are used in both tradition, although, by and large, we give more attention to qualitative methods because some quantitative studies necessitate very large samples, which is often not feasible for individual classroom teachers. One additional point needs to be made regarding the distinction between quantitative and qualitative research. These traditions can be combined in one study so that, for example, in the Willett study previously described, Willett could have included some type of survey research to gather more details about the English language use patterns of the members of the international community she was investigating. This would have provided her with some quantitative data to supplement her characterization of the international community she was studying.

Table 1.1 summarizes some of the major differences between qualitative and quantitative research. It is important to point out that the table characterizes typical features of empirical quantitative studies and ethnographic qualitative studies. Such studies represent two ends of a quantitative/qualitative continuum. It becomes clear as we discuss various methodologies that other methods fall between these two poles.

Control and Structure

Another perspective on examining the differences between qualitative and quantitative research is provided by van Lier (1988). He contends that when posing research questions and deciding on research methods, there are two important variables to consider. One is the amount of intervention or control that the researcher exerts. For example in the previously mentioned study by Chen and Graves (1995), the researchers decided to divide the university students into groups so that the groups would experience different types of introductions to reading texts. This involved a good deal of control because the students were not part of an existing class. In contrast, they could have decided to have students in four existing classes experience different types of introductions to reading texts and then observed what effect this might have on the students' understanding of the text. If they had done this, however, it would have been much more difficult to compare the effect of the four types of treatment.

A second variable that exists in selecting a research method is what van Lier calls *structuring*. In the Chen and Graves (1995) study, the researchers also wanted to know the students' reactions to these various methods of introducing a reading text. In order to answer this question they asked students to respond to an open-ended question, namely, "What kind of information do you think students should be given about a story before they read?" (p. 677). This is a relatively unstructured way to gather data. On the other hand, Chen and Graves (1995) could have decided that in place of this very open-ended question they would design a series of questions that asked students to select a particular response to each question. They might have had students select from a four-point scale from Strongly Agree to Strongly Disagree a question such as "It is important for students to be introduced to the historical background of the author before they read a text." Such questions are far more structured and make the data easier to analyze. However, this structure would have limited the kind of responses the students could have given.

Figure 1.1 summarizes how van Lier believes research methods differ. In the upper right hand box, the researcher controls the research process by designating particular groups of randomly assigned students to undertake certain activities, as was done in the Chen and Graves study. Additionally, the researcher structures the event by determining exactly what students will do. In the Chen and Graves study, there were clearly specified guidelines about what kind of information each group of students would get about the story they were about to read. In the upper left hand box, researchers structure the research by providing students with a set of questions on a survey or by describing a class they observe according to a specific coding scheme. However, there is little disruption in the regular classroom activities because the researcher does not intervene to change the composition of the class.

In the lower left hand box, the researcher does not intervene in the composition of the groups so that the students stay in the same class; in addition, the researcher does not structure the class activities in any special way. In this way, the researcher merely observes the regular classroom activities and does not restructure the activities. This is what Willett (1995) did in her study. Finally, in the lower right hand box, researchers exert control by interviewing students or asking particular students to respond to classroom questions to elicit their responses. However, little structure might be provided to the in-

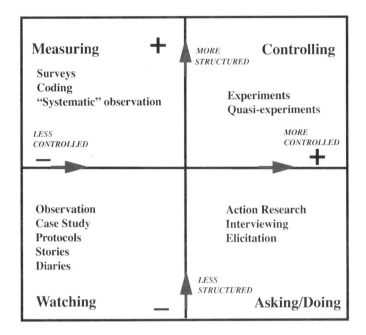

FIG. 1.1. Types of research. (Based on van Lier's typology, 1988, p. 57).

terview questions or to the questions the teachers asks the students in the class. In this way, the researcher is not structuring the activity itself.

Which type of control and structure the researcher will exert depends primarily on the research question. If, like Chen and Graves, a researcher wants to compare the effect of various types of reading text introductions, it is important to exert control and structure by deciding what will be done and how it will be done. On the other hand, if a researcher wants primarily to describe what naturally occurs in a classroom, as was done in the Willett study, then the researcher does not want to exert any control or structure over regular classroom activities. Before proceeding to examine various methods in the quantitative/qualitative continuum that can be used to study L2 teaching and learning, there are several key constructs frequently used to assess research methodologies that are important to understand.

Key Constructs

Quantitative Research

Two qualities are essential for sound research: *validity* and *reliability*. How these terms are dealt with in quantitative and qualitative research illustrates another contrast between these two traditions. To begin, we look at how these terms are used in quantitative research. There are three major types of validity: construct, external, and internal validity. *Construct validity* deals with the degree to which the instruments used in a study measure the construct that is being examined. For example, if a researcher wants to determine the degree to which language aptitude influences language learning, then the researcher needs to select some means of operationalizing the construct of language aptitude. This may involve assessing students' ability in certain skills shown to be important to language learning, such as the ability to discriminate similar sounds or to form grammatical generalizations based on language data. Typically the measures selected must appear to an outsider to be a reasonable way to assess the construct being examined.

External validity deals with the extent to which the findings of one study can be generalized to a wider population. In quantitative studies, *generalizability* is often achieved by using a random sample of a representative group of the target population. For example, if a researcher wants to make generalizations about Korean junior high students' attitudes toward communicative language teaching, the researcher would try to get a large representative sample of Korean junior high students in order to make certain that the findings of the survey can be generalized to all Korean junior high students.

Internal validity, on the other hand, deals with the degree to which the research design is such that it has controlled for variables that could influence the outcome of the study. For example, in the Chen and Graves study the researchers randomly assigned students to four groups rather than using four existing reading classes. If they had used existing classes, then there would have been the possibility that differences in reading comprehension found in the study had been caused by some aspect of the reading instruction students received rather than to the way students were prepared for the reading text.

There are two types of reliability: internal and external. *Internal reliability* relates to the extent to which someone else analyzing the same data would come up with the same results. Internal reliability can be judge through *inter-rater reliability* or *intra-rater reliability*. To determine inter-rater reliability two researchers examine the same data using the same categorization system to see to what extent they arrive at similar conclusions. For example, two researchers might score the same group of student essays using a six-point holistic scoring rubric. The degree to which the two raters agreed would indicate the level of inter-rater reliability. If a study reports an inter-rater reliability of .90, this would indicate that the two raters agreed on their rating 90% of the time and disagreed 10% of the time. Intra-rater reliability indicates the degree to which the same researcher assigns the same rating to the data on two different occasions. *External reliability*, on the other hand, deals with whether or not another researcher, undertaking a similar study, would come to the same conclusions.

Qualitative Research

These terms are defined differently in qualitative research because there is far less control and structure in qualitative research. In qualitative research, internal validity depends on what is referred to as credibility and external validity to transferability. A researcher can achieve *credibility* or internal validity by carefully recording and analyzing all of the data gathered and presenting it in a fair and unbiased manner. Lincoln and Guba (1985) describe various ways that qualitative researchers can achieve credibility. They suggest that researchers have

- prolonged engagement in the field
- persistent observation
- triangulation or the use of various sources of data and research methods in their study
- peer debriefing or discussions with peers about the research and its design and assumptions
- member checking or asking subjects in the study to check the researcher's interpretation of the data.

Transferability or external validity has to do with the degree to which the findings of a qualitative study can be applied to other contexts. The degree of transferability depends to a large degree on the similarity of the learning contexts being examined. In order for readers to determine the degree of transferability of a particular study, researchers need to provide a complete description of the participants and context of the research so that readers can determine to what extent the findings might be applicable to other contexts. Cohen, Manion, and Morrison (2000) point out that threats to external validity or transferability can include

- selection effects (where constructs selected in fact are only relevant to a certain group);
- setting effects (where the results are largely a function of their context);
- history effects (where the situations have been arrived at by unique circumstances and, therefore, are not comparable);
- construct effects (where the constructs being used are peculiar to a certain group). (p. 109)

The reliability of qualitative research depends on what is termed dependability. *Dependability* has to do with the degree to which the results reported in the study can be trusted or are reliable. In order to achieve dependability, qualitative researchers need to provide comprehensive details about their procedures and catalogue their data in such a way that others could retrieve and review the evidence they provide in their research reports. This means that in reporting qualitative studies, researchers need to provide a rich description of the students involved in the study, the context for the study, and, most importantly, all of the steps the researcher took to carry out the study. Researchers also have to be certain that in selecting examples to illustrate particular conclusions, they select representative examples from their data rather than unusual or surprising instances. As Cohen, Manion, and Morrison (2000) put it, "in qualitative research reliability can be regarded as a fit between what researchers record as data and what actually occurs in the natural setting that is being researched, i.e., a degree of accuracy and comprehensiveness of coverage" (p. 119).

Generalizability

Underlying the idea of validity and reliability in both quantitative and qualitative research is the concept of *generalizability*. In quantitative research, the degree to which a study can be generalized to other contexts can be determined through statistical procedures, which verify that the results obtained were not due to chance. Because in qualitative research, the population is generally quite limited and the amount of control exerted by the researcher is minimal, statistical measures cannot be used to achieve generalizability. Often the goal of a qualitative research is to understand what happens in one particular classroom or what the experiences are of specific language learners and teachers. As Allwright and Bailey (1991) put it, the entire topic of generalizability looks very different in qualitative research or what is sometimes called *naturalistic inquiry.*

> Instead of claiming that whatever has been discovered must be true of people in general, a naturalistic enquirer will claim that whatever understanding has been gained by an in-depth study of a real-life classroom may illuminate issues for other people. (p. 51)

Yin (2003), however, argues that qualitative researchers can arrive at analytic generalizations. Researchers achieve this by relating their findings to theoretical propositions. For example, imagine that a researcher undertook a case study of several ESL students to investigate how their motivation to learn English affected their progress in acquiring English. Through extensive interviews and observations, the researcher concludes that for these students, integrative motivation played a central role in their progress in learning English. The findings of this study would then provide further evidence of the importance of integrative motivation in language learning.

Lincoln and Guba (1985) go so far as to argue that if generalizations are taken as assertions of permanent value that are context free, then there are no real generalizations. They contend that even in quantitative inquiry, if recognition is given to the uniqueness of the local conditions and context, any generalization is a working hypothesis and not a hard and fast conclusion. As they put it,

> Local conditions, in short, make it impossible to generalize. If there is a "true" generalization, it is that there can be no generalization. And note that the "working hypotheses" are tentative both for the situation in which they are first uncovered and for other situations; there are always differences in context from situation to situation, and even the single situation differs over time. . . . Constant flux militates against conclusions that are always and forever true; they can only be said to be true under such and such conditions and circumstances. (p. 124)

Perhaps the most reasonable approach to generalizability is to accept the construct as a continuum where the more the local conditions are controlled and structured, as they are in many quantitative studies, the more the findings can be generalized to other contexts. When local conditions are not controlled and structured, as in most qualitative research, the readers themselves must determine to what extent the findings are applicable and transferable to other contexts.

Research Methods

In the following chapter on researching teachers and learners we examine various methods that can be used to study the beliefs, attitudes, and behavior of teachers and students. In general, these methods are introduced from the more controlled and structured methods to the less controlled and structured. The one exception is action research. We begin with a discussion of action research because it is a method that is directly concerned with improving L2 education and because this method is difficult to place on the continuum. This is because the amount of control and structure used in particular action research projects can vary a great deal depending on the teaching problem that is being examined. Figure 1.2 illustrates the methods we examine ranging from the more controlled and structured method of survey research to the less controlled and structured qualitative research methods. We have not included the methods we examine in chapter 3, namely interaction, discourse, and text analysis because, like action research, the amount of control and structure these methods use can differ

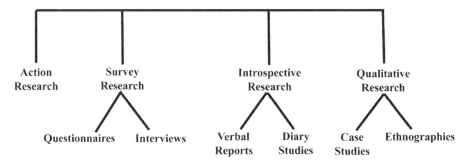

FIG. 1.2.   Continuum of research methods.

depending on the research design. For example, it is possible for a researcher using text analysis to assess the quality of student essays by counting very discrete features of student essays, thus exerting a great deal of structure on the analysis. However, researchers can also assess student essays using holistic assessment, which provides far less structure to the analysis. In the following discussion we briefly describe the central features of the methods on the continuum. Then in chapter 2, we provide an in-depth discussion of the typical procedures used in these research methods and include examples of research studies for each of the methods.

Action Research

Many teachers find action research a productive and feasible method because it can involve an investigation of their own classroom and is directly related to their classroom problems and concerns. Action research begins with teachers identifying a concrete problem they have. They then gather data to help solve the problem and, after carefully analyzing this data, undertake changes in their classroom to hopefully solve their initial problem. Some contend that action research involves more teacher reflection than research and as such should not be considered as a rigorous methodology for L2 classroom research. Others, however, argue that action research entails the essential of any research methodology: a researchable question, data gathering, and data analysis. To the extent that action research has these three essential components, it is clearly a productive method for L2 classroom research.

Surveys

The most controlled and structured method we examine in chapter 2 is survey research. Survey research is sandwiched between statistical experimental research and qualitative research because survey research can use both statistical and qualitative analysis. As we will see in chapter 2, written survey questions can be highly structured or they can be open ended. When they are more structured, they offer a productive method for gathering a large amount of very specific information on teachers' and learners' attitudes and behavior. The sample size of a survey can vary from students in one classroom to a random sample of students from a much larger population. However, statistical generalizations are only possible with a large random sample. Oral interviews can also be highly structured or open-ended. The advantage of interviews is that they allow the researcher to study individual teachers and students in much greater depth than written surveys. In all survey research, the selection of informants and the design of the questions is central to a sound research design.

Introspective Studies

In introspective studies, teachers and learners reflect on their thinking processes or their beliefs and experiences. In chapter 2 we examine two types of introspective studies: *verbal reports* and *diary studies*. In verbal reports, learners typically verbalize their thought processes while engaged in a reading or writing task. These reports can be done while the students are engaged in the process of reading or writing or after the process is completed. When the reports are retrospective they can be used with oral/aural activities. Although there are many disadvantages to using verbal reports, as is discussed in the following chapter, it is one of the few methods available for accessing the thought processes of learners. A second type of introspective methodology is diary studies. In these studies teachers or learners keep a detailed record of their teaching or learning experiences and reflect on these experiences as part of their diaries. Such studies go beyond journal keeping because they must involve a rigorous analysis of the data gathered.

Qualitative Studies

In chapter 2 we examine two particular types of qualitative studies: *case studies* and *ethnographies*. As Yin (2003) points out in his book on case study research, researchers use case studies when they believe contextual features are highly relevant to their research question. For example, a researcher might select a case study approach if he or she wants to find out if learners' progress in English is affected by whether they are in an ESL class or mainstream classroom. A second feature of case study research is that it gives attention to the many variables that might be a factor in answering the research question and thus, the researcher gathers evidence from multiple sources. For example, if a researcher were interested in examining learners' progress in ESL versus mainstream classroom, they would gather a great variety of evidence by observing students' behavior in both types of classes, gathering students' work in both contexts, and interviewing the students' teachers.

The second type of qualitative research we examine is ethnographies. Ethnographic research developed largely from anthropological research in which the overall goal was to arrive at an emic or insider's rather than an etic or outsider's perspective of what was happening. In other words, in ethnographic research, the researcher tries to interpret what is happening according to the views of people in that particular context or culture by having prolonged engagement with the participants and context. Ethnographic research can be distinguished from other types of qualitative research in several ways. First, ethnographic research involves long periods of involvement so that researchers can gain an in-depth understanding of what is being observed. Second, the researcher is a participant in the environment being examined and thus is a participant observer. As with most qualitative research, ethnographic research begins with a general rather than highly structured research question and uses multiple sources of data to investigate the question.

The choice of which method to use depends on what the researcher's objectives are. These objectives are typically specified in terms of a research question. The researcher must then specify the research design that he or she will employ to answer this question.

*   *   *

Exploring the Ideas 1.3

One of the best ways to become familiar with the various methodologies previously described is to examine studies that have used these methods. Listed below are examples of studies for each of the methods. Select one of these studies to read. As you read the study, specify the overall research question that is being examined. Then summarize the methodology of the study. Be prepared to share your summary with other class members. If you have read studies other than those listed below that exemplify one of the methods previously mentioned, you are welcome to summarize this article.

Action Research Studies

Edge, J. (2001). *Action Research.* Alexandria, VA: TESOL. (This book contains reports on various action research studies.)

PAC Journal. (This is a journal for language teachers in Asia with a focus on action research. Most of the articles report on action research studies.)

Surveys

Kamhi-Stein, L. D. (2003). Reading in two languages: How attitudes toward home language and beliefs about reading affect the behaviors of "under-prepared" L2 college readers. *TESOL Quarterly, 37*(1), 35–71. (This study uses both think aloud protocols and interviews to address the research question.)

Prodromou, L. (1992). What culture? Which culture? Cross-cultural factors in language learning. *ELT Journal, 46*(1), 39–50. (This study reports on a questionnaire of 300 Greek students to determine what culture they believe should inform classroom activities.)

Mangelsdorf, K. (1992). Peer review in the ESL composition classroom: What do the students think. *ELT Journal, 46*(3), 274–284. (This study used an open-ended questionnaire with a class of students to assess their reactions to the use of peer review in their writing class.)

Introspective Studies

Bailey, K. M. (1983). Competitiveness and anxiety in adult second language learning: Looking at and through the diary studies. In H. W. Selinger & M. H. Long (Eds.), *Classroom oriented research in second language acquisition* (pp. 67–103). Rowley, MA: Newbury House. (In this study Bailey analyzes the diaries of 10 learners of English to determine how competitiveness and anxiety influenced their language learning.)

Schmidt, R. W., & Froda, S. N. (1986). Developing basic conversational ability in a second language: A case study of an adult learner of Portuguese. In R. R. Day (Ed.), *Talking to learn: Conversation in second language acquisition* (pp. 237–326). Rowley, MA: Newbury House. (This study reports on Schmidt's use of a diary to analyze his experience learning Portuguese.)

Block, E. (1986). The comprehension strategies of second language readers. *TESOL Quarterly, 20*(3), 463–494. (This study reports on the use of think-aloud protocols to examine the reading comprehension strategies of native and nonnative English speakers enrolled in a remedial reading class.)

Gu, Y. (2003). Fine brush and freehand: The vocabulary learning art of two successful Chinese EFL learners. *TESOL Quarterly, 37*(1), 73–104. (This study reports on the use of think-aloud protocols to examine the vocabulary-learning strategies of 2 Chinese learners of English.)

Qualitative Studies

Harklau, L. (1994). ESL versus mainstream classes: Contrasting L2 learning environments. *TESOL Quarterly, 28*(2), 241–272. (In this ethnographic study, Harklau examined what 4 Chinese immigrant students gained and lost in their transition from ESL to mainstream classes.)

Leki, I. (1995). Coping strategies of ESL students in writing tasks across the curriculum. *TESOL Quarterly, 29*(2), 235–260. (This case study examined the writing strategies 5 ESL students developed to cope with the writing demands they encountered in their academic classes.)

Willett, J. (1995). Becoming first graders in an L2: An ethnographic study of L2 socialization. *TESOL Quarterly, 29*(3), 473–504. (This ethnographic study reports on the participation patterns of ESL children placed in a first-grade mainstream classroom.)

*   *   *

Research Questions and Designs

Examining Beliefs

The first step in generating a research question is to carefully consider your own beliefs about L2 teaching and learning because these beliefs will influence the framing of the research question and your choice of research design. Imagine, for example, that you are very interested in the general topic of L2 writing. In much of the existing research on L2 writing, one of two basic ideologies informs research. One ideology views L2 writing as essentially an individual skill, which, if developed, has cognitive benefits. Street (1984) labels this perspective as an *autonomous model of literacy*. The second ideology assumes that writing is above all a social practice that connects people across a range of time and experiences. Street (1984) labels this perspective as the *ideological model of literacy*. In the autonomous model, writing is approached basically as an individual process whereas in the ideological model it is seen as a social process. These two ideologies, of course, are not mutually exclusive. However, many researchers select one perspective over another.

For example, one early study that supports the autonomous model of literacy is a study by Raimes (1985) who wanted to examine the composing processes of unskilled ESL students. In order to discover the strategies these students used, she had unskilled ESL students report on their thinking processes as they wrote an ESL essay. She then categorized the strategies they used in order to determine if there were any patterns in the way these students approached the composing process. In terms of ideology, Raimes approached L2 literacy as essentially an individual cognitive process. Leki (1995), on the other hand, chose to examine how the larger academic context influences how L2 writers acquire the forms and attitudes necessary to write successfully in their particular academic field. In order to examine some of the social factors involved in writing academic essays, Leki undertook an in-depth observation of several ESL graduate and undergraduate students to determine how their overall academic experience influenced their writing in their own disciplines. By doing so, Leki approached literacy as a social practice embedded in a particular academic context.

Studies such as these illustrate that the research question one asks typically reflects a particular ideological stance. This ideology greatly affects what questions the researcher believes are important to answer. Why then is it important for you to clarify your own beliefs about L2 teaching and learning before generating your research question? The primary reason is that by recognizing your own beliefs you are able to determine your own biases and preferences. There is indeed nothing wrong in supporting a particular view of L2 teaching and learning, but by explicitly stating these beliefs you can understand the assumptions and biases you bring to your research. Perhaps the most productive way for you to clarify your own beliefs is to review studies done on a topic you are interested in and identify the assumptions the authors are making about L2 teaching and learning in designing the study the way they did. Then consider whether or not you support these assumptions.

Specifying a Research Question

In determining your research question, the first step is to specify an area of inquiry you are interested in. This interest may be initiated by a particular problem or challenge you are facing in your classroom, as is typically done in action research. However, the inquiry can also begin with a topic you are interested in for its own sake. This interest can come from your reading in L2 education literature or from your own experiences in teaching or learning a second language. In determining a research question, you might begin with a general research question, such as "What are the characteristics of effective group work tasks?" or "Is guessing words from context a productive strategy for vocabulary learning?" In formulating a more specific question, you should then do reading in the general area to find out what studies exist on the topic.

*   *   *

Exploring the Ideas, 1.4

In order to help you determine a research question you are interested in studying, list questions that interest you on three or four of the topics listed here. If there are other topics that interest you, add these to the list. For example, under the topic of group work, you might list questions such as "For what purposes do students use their first language in undertaking group work?" or "What are students' attitudes toward the use of group work?"

• Student Motivation
• Learning Strategies
• Teacher Questions

- Teacher Feedback
- Classroom Texts
- Group Work
- Teaching Grammar
- Teaching Reading
- Teaching Writing
- Teaching Listening
- Teaching Speaking

*   *   *

Exploring the Ideas, 1.5

Select one of the questions you listed in *Exploring the Ideas, 1.4* that you want to research. Then read three to four professional articles on the topic. After doing so, try to frame a general research question you could explore on this topic. Finally, list the kinds of data you would gather to answer your research question. Write up your findings by describing

- The research area you are interested in exploring and why you are interested in this topic
- The findings of the articles you read on the topic
- The general research question you would like to address
- The type of data you would gather to answer your question

*   *   *

Developing a Research Design

Once you determine your general research question, you need to plan the steps you will follow to answer this question. Cohen, Manion, and Morrison (2000) delineate a four stage framework for planning a research project that may be helpful to you in planning your research. These stages involve

1. orienting decisions;
2. research design and methodology;
3. data analysis;
4. presenting and reporting the results. (p. 74)

Orienting decisions are strategic decisions in that they describe the general nature of the research. Some of the questions that need to be addressed in this area are

- What are the general aims of the research?
- Who is the likely audience for the research?
- What are the constraints on the research?
- What is the time frame for the research?
- What ethical issues need to be dealt with in undertaking the research?
- What resources are required for the research?

Research design and methodology issues are basically tactical decisions in that they establish the practicalities of the research. Some of the questions that need addressing in this area are

- What is the main methodology of the research?
- How will validity and reliability be dealt with?
- What kinds of data will be gathered, and how will it be gathered?
- Who will undertake the research?

In planning the *data analysis*, researchers need to decide how they will analyze the data that is gathered. In the following chapters we describe various ways that qualitative data can be analyzed. In general, however, the process of data analysis in qualitative research is inductive in nature with researchers reviewing the data gathered in order to discover patterns.

The final stage of research planning is *presenting and reporting the results*. In this stage researchers need to consider questions such as the following:

- Who will be the audience for the report?
- When will the report be written?
- Where will the report be shared?
- How will the data be presented?

We discuss various options for presenting and reporting research results in chapter 4.

* * *

Exploring the Ideas, 1.6

Using the research question you described earlier, answer the questions just listed under Orienting Decisions and Research Design and Methodology. In answering the question regarding constraints, consider what problems you anticipate in undertaking the project and describe how you intend to handle these problems. For example, it may be that your research project must be completed in a particular time frame or that you have limited access to L2 classrooms or a limited budget to gather data. Describe how you would deal with these constraints in undertaking your research project. In answering the question on the ethical issues that need to be addressed in your study, read the following section on Ethical Research.

*   *   *

ETHICAL RESEARCH

Respecting Participants

In 1982, Labov raised several important issues regarding the role of linguists in undertaking research. Among these was what he termed the *principle of debt incurred*, which he described in the following manner.

> An investigator who has obtained linguistic data from members of a speech community has an obligation to use the knowledge based on that data for the benefit of the community, when it has need of it. (p. 134)

For our purposes, this principle implies that those doing research in a language classroom have an obligation to use the data they gather to increase the effectiveness of the teaching and learning of that community of learners.

In their book on issues of power and method in language research, Cameron, Frazer, Harvey, Rampton, and Richardson (1992) raise a related point when they argue that empowering research needs to be research *on*, *for*, and *with*. They believe that teachers should not merely do research on students or classrooms but rather do research *for* the benefit of students and teachers and ideally *with* learners and other teachers in an interactive framework.

The authors discuss three points they believe need to be recognized in undertaking empowering research.

- First "persons are not objects and should not be treated as objects" (p. 23). In other words, researchers need to approach learners and teachers in their studies as full human beings and not merely as research objects.
- Second, "subjects have their own agendas and research should try to address them" (p. 23). Researchers are powerful in that they decide what will be researched and which activities to undertake in doing this research. However, individuals who participate in their studies have their own agendas about what issues they would like to see investi-

gated. Researchers should try to discover these objectives and, if possible, include them in their research.

- Finally, "if knowledge is worth having, it is worth sharing" (p. 24). The expert knowledge that comes from doing research should be shared not just with other interested professionals but also with the individuals who participated in the research.

Following Institutional Guidelines

A concern for promoting empowering and ethical research in applied linguistics has resulted in various organizations developing guidelines that must be adhered to when human subjects are involved. Most institutions of higher learning have a set of such guidelines. If you are a graduate student or teacher it is essential that before you undertake any classroom research, you consult and follow the guidelines of your institution. Typically these guidelines spell out under what conditions researchers must get informed consent from their participants. In general, anonymous written surveys do not require informed consent. In addition, when participants in a study are minors, informed consent forms should be obtained from parents or guardians.

Many institutions adhere to guidelines specified by the United States *Code of Federal Regulations*, 45CFR.46.116, which specify that for consent forms to be valid, they must be based on the following elements.

- The participant must be COMPETENT to begin the informed consent process. If the participant is not competent because of age, illness, incapacity, or any other reason, special provisions apply, or the participant may not be included in the research.
- The research team must DISCLOSE all relevant information to the potential participant. The information must be sufficient to allow the potential participant to decide whether to participate. It is generally accepted that the potential participant must be given the following information: the purpose of the study; nature of the procedure; reasonable alternatives to the proposed intervention; and risks, benefits, and uncertainties of each possible intervention.
- The participant must COMPREHEND the information. The research team must evaluate the potential participant's ability to understand the proposed intervention in the study.
- The participant must AGREE to the proposed intervention in the research study.
- The participant's agreement must be VOLUNTARY and free from coercion.

Source: National Institutes of Health (NIH, 2002, p. 29)

Because participants should be competent in the language used in the informed consent statement, with less proficient speakers of English, it is preferable to have the informed consent written in the individual's mother tongue. Based on the criteria previously listed, an informed consent form should contain the following.

- A statement indicating that the researcher is conducting research in which the individual will be asked to participate and that the researcher may use the data he or she gathers in future publications.
- A statement of the purpose of the research project, the procedures the researcher will follow, what the participants will be asked to do, and how the identity of the participants will be protected.
- A statement of the risks and benefits there might be for the participants.
- A statement indicating that the individual's participation is completely voluntary and that he or she may withdraw from the project at any time with no penalty.

Researchers must get from each of the participants a signed consent form that outlines the specific terms of their agreement. Often university or other institutional guidelines on human subject research contain sample consent forms that can be modified to suit the particular purposes of the individual researcher. Following such guidelines and getting consent forms is important for several reasons. First and most importantly, it is one way of demonstrating respect for the individuals involved in a research project. Second, most institutions involved in research projects require it. And finally, it is necessary for publication of the findings of a study in a refereed journal.

* * *

Exploring the Ideas, 1.7

Obtain the human subject guidelines your institution currently uses. Bring a copy of these guidelines to class to share with your classmates. If your proposed research project will require consent forms, prepare a draft of the consent form you intend to use. If possible, share this draft with your classmates for their input and suggestions.

* * *

Gaining Access

If you anticipate your research project will involve teachers and learners in a particular school, you should make initial contact with key administrators as soon as possible in order to get permission to work there. Contact the principal of the school to explain your research, answer his or her questions about the project, and obtain permission to work in the school. Once you get this permission, contact the teachers you would like to include in your project. Again you should personally contact these individuals to explain your project and ask for their cooperation in the project. Once this initial contact has been made, you can ask potential participants to sign informed consent forms. Be certain to spend all the time needed to explain the goals of your project and answer any questions participants may have. The more rapport you can establish with administrators and teachers before you begin collecting data, the fewer problems you will have later.

If your project involves minors, try to get permission from parents as soon as possible. Be certain in your initial contact with the parents to inform them of all the essential information contained in the informed consent statement: the purpose of your research, the role their children will have in this project, the risks and benefits that come with their children participating in the project, and how their children's anonymity will be preserved.

If your research involves interviewing individual teachers or students or including them in a case study, be certain to contact individuals you would like to participate as soon as possible in order to explain the project and obtain informed consent statements. Again take time to fully answer all of their questions and establish a good relationship with them. In most cases, you can expect there will be attrition due to participants dropping out or moving to other areas. For this reason, it is good to get permission from more participants than you believe you will need. The sooner you get permission the better because your research cannot begin until this step is taken. The most important point to remember, however, is to treat your participants with respect and to make certain that your research will benefit them.

SUMMARY

We began this chapter by discussing the benefits that can be gained from doing research and pointing out some of the practical problems researchers face in doing research. The chapter then described various purposes that research can serve. Whereas the goal of basic research is to contribute to general knowledge, applied research has direct implications for social problems. We then distinguished qualitative and quantitative research traditions, noting how these traditions differ in their assumptions about reality, the role of the researcher, the purpose of the research, and the research design. Finally, we described various research methods that are commonly used in L2 classroom research.

In discussing research questions, we emphasized that researchers need to begin by designating an area of L2 teaching and learning they are interested in and clarifying their own biases and beliefs. Then they need to review existing research in this area in order to formulate a research question. Once they have specified a research question, they need to plan their research design, specifying their research methodology and time line. They also need to consider the practical problems that exist in doing the research project. We closed the chapter by arguing that it is extremely important for researchers to respect the people they study and to consider how they can share their findings so they benefit the participants.

FURTHER READING

Basic Methodology Texts on L2 Educational Research

Allwright, D., & Bailey, K. M. (1991). *Focus on the language classroom.* Cambridge, UK: Cambridge University Press.

Brown, J. D. (1988). *Understanding research in second language.* Cambridge, UK: Cambridge University Press.

Brown, J. D., & Rodgers, T. S. (2002). *Doing second language research.* Oxford, UK: Oxford University Press.

Chaudron, C. (1988). *Second language classrooms: Research on teaching and learning.* Cambridge, UK: Cambridge University Press.

Cohen, L., Manion, L., & Morrison, K. (2000). *Research methods in education.* London: Routledge Falmer.

Johnson, D. (1992). *Approaches to research in second language learning.* New York: Longman.

McDonough, J., & McDonough, S. (1997). *Research methods for English language teachers.* London: Arnold.

Nunan, D. (1992). *Research methods in language learning.* Cambridge, UK: Cambridge University Press.

van Lier, L. (1988). *The classroom and the language learner.* London: Longman.

Researching Teachers and Learners

In this chapter we examine the following questions:

- What are the assumptions and procedures of research methods commonly used to examine the behavior, beliefs, and thoughts of second language teachers and learners?
- What are examples of such research studies?

We examine these methods from the more controlled and structured methods to the less controlled and structured. Hence, we begin with survey research with a focus on written questionnaires and oral interviews, followed by introspective research including verbal reports and diary studies, and ending with qualitative research with attention to case studies and ethnographies. Before doing so, however, we discuss the assumptions and procedures of action research. We start with this method for two reasons: First, it is a method that, by definition, is directly concerned with promoting more effective L2 teaching and learning; and second, it cannot be easily placed on a quantitative/qualitative continuum because the amount of control and structure used in action research studies can vary greatly.

ACTION RESEARCH

Defining Action Research

Action research has been defined in a number of ways but, as Nunan (1992) points out, it typically has three major characteristics: It is carried out by practitioners (i.e., classroom teachers), it is collaborative, and it is aimed at changing things. Burns (1999) expands on these characteristics, maintaining that action research exemplifies the following features.

1. Action research is contextual, small-scale and localized—it identifies and investigates problems within a specific situation.
2. It is evaluative and reflective as it aims to bring about change and improvement in practice.
3. It is participatory as it provides for collaborative investigation by teams of colleagues, practitioners and researchers.
4. Changes in practice are based on the collection of information or data which provides the impetus for change. (p. 30)

There are several features of this definition that are important to highlight. First, action research, as the name implies, involves *action* in that it seeks to bring about change, specifically in local educational contexts. It is also *research* because it entails the collection and analysis of data. Finally, it is *participatory and collaborative* in that teachers work together to examine their own classrooms.

The concept of action research developed out of the progressive education movement of the early 20th century when educators like John Dewey challenged the prevalent reliance on scientific research methods. Dewey believed it was essential for researchers, practitioners, and others in the educational community to become collectively involved in educational research in order to address common educational problems. Later the theoretical foundations of action research were influenced by the work of Kurt Lewin, a social psychologist, who in the 1940s outlined a method for dealing with social problems that consisted of a four-stage action cycle: planning, acting, observing, and reflecting. In this cycle researchers

- develop a plan of critically informed action to improve what is already happening,
- act to implement the plan,
- observe the effects of the critically informed action in the context in which it occurs, and
- reflect on these effects as the basis for further planning, subsequent critically informed action and so on, through a succession of stages. (Kemmis & McTaggart, as cited in Burns, 1999, p. 32)

Kemmis and McTaggart (1992) contend that there are several reasons why action research is far more than teachers reflecting on their own problems.

- It is *not* the usual thinking teachers do when they think about their teaching. Action research is more systematic and collaborative in collecting evidence on which to base rigorous group reflection.
- It is *not* simply problem-solving. Action research involves problem-posing, not just problem-solving. It does not start from a view of "problems" as pathologies. It is motivated by a quest to improve and understand the world by changing it and learning how to improve it from the effects of the changes made.
- It is *not* research done on other people. Action research is research by particular people on their own work, to help them improve what they do, including how they work with and for others. . . .
- Action research is *not* "the scientific method" applied to teaching. There is not just one view of "the scientific method"; there are many. . . . (pp. 21–22)

As Burns (1999) notes, because action research is often judged in relation to empirical paradigms and methods, it has been criticized for "its inability to test hypotheses or to establish cause and effect relationships, for its resistance to the basic techniques and procedures of research and for its lack of generalisability" (p. 27). Some even question whether or not action research should be considered as a viable research method. However, Nunan (1992), while recognizing the problems of reliability and validity in action research, contends that action research should be taken as a research method in its own right if it addresses questions of interest to other practitioners, generates data, and contains analysis and interpretation. The value of action research is that, if undertaken with rigor, it can supply local knowledge regarding problems in L2 teaching and learning and suggest ways for addressing these problems. In order to clarify how this can be done, we turn now to an examination of the procedures for an action research cycle.

Action Research Procedures

Cohen, Manion, and Morrison (2000) provide a clear description of the stages of action research. These stages are as follows.

- Stage 1: Researchers *identify, evaluate, and formulate a problem* that is viewed as critical to their everyday teaching. This problem need not be restricted to a particular class but could involve a system change such as curriculum innovations in a school system.
- Stage 2: Researchers *consult with other interested parties*—teachers, other researchers, and administrators—in order to focus the problem more clearly and perhaps suggest the cause of the problem. This stage is cru-

cial because it involves the clarification of the objectives and assumptions of the study.

- Stage 3: Researchers *review research literature* to find out what can be learned from comparable studies.
- Stage 4: Based on their reading, researchers may *modify or redefine the initial statement of the problem*, which may take the form of a set of objectives or a testable hypothesis. They also explicitly state the assumptions underlying the project.
- Stage 5: Researchers *specify the research design* including the participants, choice of materials, and procedures.
- Stage 6: Researchers *clarify how the project will be evaluated* with an understanding that this evaluation will be continuous.
- Stage 7: Researchers *implement the project* undertaking the data collection process.
- Stage 8: Researchers *analyze the data, draw inferences, and evaluate the project.*

During the final stage of analysis and reflection, researchers may decide to implement another cycle, thus continuing the research process.

Action Research Studies

One example of an action research study is Cowie (2001) who describes his experience of using a series of action research cycles to improve his feedback on students' essays in an undergraduate writing class in a public liberal arts university in Japan. Whereas his investigation exemplifies most of the stages previously listed, it is lacking in the collaborative process that is central to many definitions of action research.

Cowie's motivation for studying his own teaching context was his dissatisfaction with his written feedback on student essays (*Stage 1*, initial formulation of the problem). After examining some of the existing literature on teacher feedback (*Stage 3*, review of the literature), Cowie decided that his initial focus would be to examine how the way in which he gave written feedback and the type of feedback he gave could motivate students to rewrite their essays (*Stage 4*, modify the initial problem). His attention to this question spanned 3 years in which he considered various ways to provide feedback, collected classroom data, and reflected on the effect of the changes he made. In first year he gave written feedback to student essays based on four main principles: He would respond to students' ideas, try to be positive, give priority to global concerns, and provide a limited focus on form. As a way of assessing his procedure for written feedback he examined his postcourse evaluations, some of the student essays, and administrative records of attendance and essays submitted. He found that of the 140 essays he had responded to, only 11 were rewritten (*Stages 7 and 8*, implementing the project, analyzing the data, drawing inferences, and evaluating the project).

In the second year, he decided to try to give feedback through audiotaped comments, believing that this would decrease the amount of time he spent marking papers, give students more comments and listening practice, and motivate students to rewrite more. He then transcribed some of his tapes and found that although he could say between 120 and 150 words a minute, he could only write about 70 words in 2 minutes (*Stages 7 and 8*, implement the project, collect data, draw inferences). He also found that in his written comments, his end comments tended to be 50–100 words whereas his audiotaped comments ranged from 200 to 500 words. Hence, he was providing more feedback with the use of audiotapes. In order to determine to what extent the audiotapes were an effective way to provide students with feedback, he gathered students' written comments on the use of audiotapes. He also noted how many papers were rewritten (*Stages 7 and 8*, implementing the project, analyzing the data, drawing inferences and evaluating the project). He continued his attention to feedback in the third year by explaining to students he was giving them tapes because he wanted to encourage them to rewrite their essays, and he told them how they might effectively use the tapes.

Cowie's assessment of his use of feedback in his writing class exemplifies central features of action research cycles. First, it began with his identifying a classroom problem. Next he considered ways to improve his feedback, made changes to his feedback procedures, and examined what effect these changes had in his classroom. In short, he undertook a series of cycles, hoping in each instance to improve the effectiveness of his written feedback.

*   *   *

Exploring the Ideas, 2.1

Review an action research study. You may use one of the studies cited in chapter 1.

Action Research Studies

> Edge, J. (2001). *Action Research*. Alexandria, VA: TESOL. (This book contains reports on various action research studies.)
>
> *PAC Journal.* (This journal is a journal for language teachers in Asia with a focus on action research. Most of the articles report on action research studies.)

As you read the article, evaluate the study according to the eight stages of an action research cycle listed here. Which stages are present and which are lacking? Are there any ways in which you think the research design could have been improved?

$$* \quad * \quad *$$

Exploring the Ideas, 2.2

In his case studies of L2 classrooms, Richards (1998) includes a series of descriptions of classroom problems faced by practitioners in ESL and EFL contexts.

Study the case study that follows and then specify the series of steps you would take if you were to implement an action research cycle to address the problem that is described. Be certain to indicate what action you would take, why you would take this action, what data you would collect, and how you would evaluate the data.

The teaching problem identified by Bond (1998) occurred in an English for academic program in a large urban university in southeastern U.S. The class involved was a writing class that met twice a week for 2 hours with 15 members from various countries. The writing assignments for the course were based on reading assignments from a U.S. history textbook. Bonds identified his problem in the following manner.

The problem I was having in my class had to do with my attempt to do group (mostly pair) writing in class and with the fact that with such a diverse group of students, it did not always run smoothly. We did a good deal of writing and editing in pairs, calling these sessions writing workshops. Students generally read each other's plans for an essay or one for the drafts of an essay they had worked on in class or at home. They then edited each other's work by writing or making comments about the content (facts), organization (logical progression), or English (e.g., complete sentences) of the work. My main reason for requiring this pair work was that I wanted to help the students to get ideas from and function as models for each other by reading each other's work and getting feedback on their own. I also wanted students to get into the habit of reading critically so that this critical reading might be used to better write and edit their work.

Some students seemed very positive about group writing and editing in class. . . . Students like this were very enthusiastic any time they found out that we were going to do group writing in the class. Other students, such as one Russian student who wrote, "Also I prefer to work in class by myself. I don't like to work with someone," were much less enthusiastic and showed little cooperative spirit in such groups.

Whether this lack of enthusiasm on the part of some students was due to the great variety of cultural backgrounds in the class, or simply the result of differences in personal learning styles is difficult to say. What concerned me was that often learners with completely different types of learning styles would be paired together if I did the pairing randomly. It did neither learner any good when one who was very enthusiastic about working with others was paired with another student who believed that the best way to improve writing was concentrated personal effort, and thought that group work was mostly distracting and a waste of time. The result of this kind of combination was two very frustrated learners. (pp. 176–177)

* * *

SURVEY RESEARCH

Surveys

Defining Surveys

According to Brown (2001), language surveys are any studies "that gather data on the characteristics and views of informants about the nature of language or language learning through the use of oral interviews or written questionnaires" (p. 2). In this chapter, we define surveys more narrowly as written questionnaires. We do so for two reasons. First, surveys are often thought of as exclusively written questionnaires, and secondly, the design and data analysis of interviews are generally quite different from surveys. Hence, we deal with interviews in a separate section of the chapter.

As Dornyei (2003) points out, surveys can provide three types of information:

- *Factual information*—Factual questions are used to find out more about the characteristics of individual teachers and learners (e.g., students' age, gender, ethnicity, language background, proficiency level, etc.).
- *Behavioral information*—Behavioral questions seek to find out what students or teachers have done or regularly do in terms of their language teaching and learning. Such questions are frequently used on language learning strategy questionnaires in which students are asked, for example, to report how often they look up unfamiliar words in a dictionary or make an outline before they write an essay.
- *Attitudinal information*—Attitudinal questions seek to find out more about the opinions, beliefs, or interests of teachers or learners. These questions are often used in needs analysis research when researchers want to gather information on such topics as what learning goals students have or what skill areas they are most interested in.

As Dornyei (2003) notes, surveys provide a very efficient means for researchers to gather a good deal of information in a short time with little cost. As such, surveys are a particularly effective way for teachers to find out more about the background, habits, and preferences of their students, information which they can then use in curriculum development. However, surveys have disadvantages. For one thing, teachers and students can provide unreliable information. Students, for example, may report that they frequently use certain language learning strategies because they believe that is what they should report. Surveys can also result in very superficial or simple responses. For example, if a researcher wants to find out more about how language learners use the target language outside of the classroom, he or she could ask a series of questions regarding with whom students use English and for what purposes. However, if a student reports that he or she rarely uses the target language with his or her family, we learn little about under what circumstances and with which family members a student might use the target language at home.

Designing Surveys

Selecting Respondents.   In designing a survey, the primary questions the researcher needs to address are what is the purpose of the survey and who will take the survey. Teachers who wish to find out more about the preferences and needs of their students in order to design a curriculum will give the survey to their students. On the other hand, a researcher who wants to study the reactions of typical Japanese high school students to the use of communicative methods in their English classes needs to get a representative sample of this large group of students. To get a representative sample, researchers use a *random sample* in which every individual in a particular population has an equal chance of being included in the survey. In order to ensure that each individual has an equal chance of being included, Brown (2001) suggests that researchers

1. Identify clearly the population of interest in the survey.
2. Assign an identification number to each individual in the population.
3. Choose the members of the sample on the basis of a table of random numbers. (p. 72)

The table of random numbers is a list of numbers that has no systematic pattern, thus ensuring that all individuals have an equal chance of being selected.

In some cases, a researcher may want to use a *stratified random sample* that controls for salient features of the target population such as gender, academic status, and home location. Stratified random samples should be used if the population is quite heterogeneous or when researchers are using the strata as the basis for their analysis. In order to obtain a stratified random sample, a researcher should

1. Identify clearly the population of interest in the survey.
2. Identify the salient characteristics of the population (called **strata**).
3. Select members randomly from each of the strata in the population (using a table of random numbers or some other procedure. . . .)
4. Examine the resulting sample to make sure that it has about the same proportions of each characteristic as the original population. (Brown, 2001, p. 73)

Sometimes it is difficult to get a true random sample, so researchers use what is termed a *sample of convenience*, that is, researchers use participants they are able to get access to. If a sample of convenience is used, it is important to try to select a group that is in some way representative of the larger population. In the case of Japanese high school students, for example, the researcher would want to include a representative population of male and female, rural and urban schools, and of high-achieving and low-achieving schools and so on.

Writing Questions.   What questions to ask on a survey should be decided on the basis of a theoretically-driven list of topics that the researcher wants to address in the survey. For example, if a researcher is designing a survey to find out to what extent students use reading strategies, the researcher would likely decide to include items that deal both with metacognitive strategies, such as planning and monitoring, as well as cognitive strategies, such as inferencing and predicting. Once these areas are determined, then the researcher can begin to write individual survey items. Survey questions can take a variety of forms. The two main types of questions are *open-ended* and *close-ended questions*.

Open-ended questions

Open-ended questions allow respondents to write in their own answers. They typically take one of two forms: *fill-in* or *short answer*. Fill-in questions are often used in demographic questions when, for example, a researcher wants to know what languages a learner speaks or how long they have been in a country. Short-answer questions, on the other hand, can be used to encourage learners to give detailed information regarding some aspect of L2 teaching or learning. For example, students might be asked to describe the type of classroom activities they find the most helpful or to describe what kinds of things they like to read in the target language.

Close-ended questions

Close-ended questions require the respondent to choose one of several specified answers and can also take a variety of forms. One possibility is an *alternative-answer* question in which students have to select from one of several options such as yes or no, or true or false. This format could be used to find out more about the learning strategies that students use such as the following question.

Do you keep a vocabulary log?　　　YES　　NO

Alternative-answer questions could also be used to select demographic information such as whether a student attended a public or private school or how long they studied English (e.g., less than one year; 1–2 years; 2–5 years; more than 5 years).

One of the most popular formats of close-ended questions is the *Likert-scale* question in which students or teachers are asked to select one of several categories by circling or checking their response. Typically these questions ask participants to rate an item according to some dimension such as importance, interest, or usefulness, as, for example:

Circle the response that best describes your interest in the following types of reading materials.

	Very Interesting	Interesting	Somewhat Interesting	Not Interesting
Magazines	1	2	3	4
Novels	1	2	3	4
Comics	1	2	3	4
Web Pages	1	2	3	4

One controversy that surrounds the use of Likert-scale questions is whether there should be an even or odd number of options. If there is an odd number of options, it may be that students consistently choose the middle option as a way to avoid taking a clear stand on a topic. Because of this, some advocate the use of an even number scale.

A third type of close-ended question is a *checklist format* in which teachers or students are asked to check all the answers that apply to their situation. For example, students might be asked to check all of the kinds of materials they find interesting to read, or teachers might be asked to check all of the types of grammar activities they use. Finally, teachers and students can be asked to *rank answers* to a particular question. For example, students could be asked to rank which skill they feel most confident about—reading, writing, speaking or listening. In designing ranking items it is best to keep the number of ranked items fairly limited, from perhaps three to five items. Otherwise it becomes difficult for respondents to rank the items. One disadvantage of ranking items is that it is difficult to summarize the results from such questions because it is not possible to get the average response on an item as can be done with Likert-scale items.

There are advantages and disadvantages to both close-ended and open-ended questions. Close-ended questions allow for more uniformity of responses and are easy to answer, code, and analyze. On the other hand, they provide a narrower range of answers and can be difficult to write. In contrast, open-ended questions can provide richer data and are relatively easy to write, but they can be extremely difficult to code and analyze.

Wording Questions. Typically, survey questions should be short so that respondents can read them quickly and answer them easily. Questions also need to be written at a language level that students understand. This can be particularly challenging if the researcher is surveying students with limited English proficiency. One way to deal with this problem is to write the questionnaire in the mother tongue, if this is a feasible alternative. Brown (2001) points out several types of questions that should be avoided including the following.

1. *Negative questions.* Because they can be confusing, negative questions should be avoided (e.g., "Spelling words correctly in English is not difficult for me." TRUE/FALSE).

2. *Doubled-barreled questions.* Double-barreled questions ask two or more questions at the same time and thus they should be avoided (e.g., "In our class we should spend more time on reading and less time on speaking." AGREE/DISAGREE).

3. *Leading questions.* Leading questions are questions that encourage learners to respond in a certain way (e.g., "Do you use the effective learning strategy of keeping a vocabulary log?" YES NO).

4. *Embarrassing questions.* Questions that respondents may find embarrassing to answer for social or cultural reasons should be avoided (e.g., "What is the literacy level of your parents?" "What is your father's occupation?").

5. *Biased questions.* Questions that are biased in terms of race, gender, religion, or nationality should not be used (e.g., "I like working in small groups with women because they are better language learners than men.").

Within the survey itself, the questions should be ordered in some logical way. One way to order the questions could be by topic so that, for example, questions involving one particular skill could be put together. Another way to order a survey might be by the type of question so that all of the questions that use a particular type of close-ended question could be put together. Finally, questions could be grouped by the function of the question so that all the questions that deal with factual information as opposed to opinion information would be listed together.

Final Survey Form.   The final form of the survey should be attractive in its layout and carefully edited with these parts.

- First a short statement that describes the *purpose of the survey* and who is conducting the survey. A teacher, for example, might begin a student survey with a short statement, such as, "I am conducting this survey to find out more about your interests and needs in learning English so that I can use this information to design classroom activities that meet your needs."
- Next there should be *instructions* regarding what the respondents should do. Typically these instructions emphasize that there are no right or wrong answers; also generally students are told that their responses are confidential and anonymous and will not affect their grades.
- The *questions* themselves should appear in some organized manner with specific instructions for each part of the questionnaire. Often the demographic information appears at the end of the survey so that the survey can open with questions that are of more interest to the respondents.
- The questionnaire should end with a brief *thank you* to the respondents for answering the survey.

Dornyei (2003) offers several additional suggestions regarding the form of the final questionnaire including the following.

1. In general the questionnaire should be no more than four pages and take no more than 30 minutes to complete.
2. In deciding the content of the questionnaire, begin by generating a theoretically driven list of the main areas to be covered.
3. In the initial instructions be certain to state the topic and importance of the questionnaire, the individual sponsoring the questionnaire, a request for honest responses, and a promise of confidentiality.
4. In the specific instructions exemplify rather than merely explain how to answer the questions.
5. Try to make the opening questions particularly involving.
6. Be certain that the questionnaire has a clear, logical, and well-marked structure.

7. Avoid open-ended questions that require lengthy answers.

8. Open-ended questions are least intrusive toward the end of the questionnaire.

9. Try to have an attractive and professional design for the questionnaire by not overcrowding pages, using various typefaces, and good paper quality.

10. At the end of the questionnaire be certain to thank participants for their participation.

Piloting a Survey.   The value of a survey is increased by piloting the instrument, that is, giving the survey to a group of teachers or learners who are similar to the group that will be surveyed. The purpose of piloting a survey is to find out what problems exist in the clarity of the directions and which items might be confusing or difficult. If the survey is going to be given to only one or two classes of students, then having three or four student pilot the survey is sufficient. If, on the other hand, the survey will be given to many students, then a larger pilot sample is needed in order to analyze the kinds of responses that are given.

Once you receive the responses, you should do an item analysis of the questions on the survey. An item analysis involves looking for several types of problems with the design of the questions.

- First, check items to which almost everyone gave the same response. Whereas it could be that this result reflects the true state of affairs, it may be that the way in which the question is worded leads everyone to respond in the same manner.

- Second, look for whether or not any items tended to be omitted by a large number of respondents. If so, this item may be confusing or difficult to answer.

Reliability.   In designing a survey, as in all research, it is essential for researchers to strive for reliability. In order to assure the reliability of a survey, several measures can be used. First, the same survey can be given on two occasions to the same individuals. Then the researcher can check to see how consistently the respondents gave the same response to the same item. The second way of assuring reliability is to have two forms of a survey and have individuals take both forms. The consistency of response on these two forms could again be checked. The final way to achieve reliability is to check the internal consistency of responses in a survey. In this case, if a survey contains several items that ask similar questions but in different forms, then the researcher can check to see how consistently the respondents have answered these questions.

Compiling and Displaying Survey Results

Close-Ended Questions.   In compiling survey results the first thing a researcher needs to do is to decide on coding categories. Often with close-ended questions, responses are given a particular numerical value. Numerical scales can be of three types.

- A *nominal scale* categorizes constructs that have no numerical value such as ethnic background or gender. For example, in coding the demographic information included on a survey, a researcher could assign a 1 to male and a 2 to female, even though these categories have no numerical value.
- An *ordinal or ranked scale* is similar to a nominal scale but involves ranked numbers. For example, if a questionnaire asked students to rank the skills—reading, writing, listening and speaking—in the order of their importance to the student, this would result in a ranked scale.
- *Interval scales* also rank numbers but describe scales that have an equal distance between each number as, for example, in test scores where it is assumed that a score of 100 is twice as good as a score of 50. Often attitude scales on a questionnaire are also treated as interval scales. For example, frequently when Likert-scales are used, each response is given a number (e.g., strongly agree = 1, agree = 2, disagree = 3, and strongly disagree = 4) and these numbers are treated as interval scales.

Recognizing the difference in these scales becomes important when we discuss how survey results can be analyzed.

Once you assign a numerical code to your data, the data needs to be recorded in some fashion. The best way to do this is in some type of a table in which you identify the respondents in the left-hand column and use the rows in the table to list the participant's response to each item. This can be a tedious process, which is most easily done by having one person read each participant's response while another records the information, often on some type of computer spreadsheet. When any data is missing from an individual questionnaire, be certain to leave a blank space.

Once the information is compiled in a table, it needs to be displayed in some way. There are several possible alternatives.

- One is to simply report the *frequency* of each response. Hence, in the example of having students rank the importance of each skill, one could simply describe how many students ranked writing as one, how many ranked listening as one, and so on.
- A second alternative is to describe the results in *percentages*. If researchers choose to describe the results in terms of frequency or percentages

they could also display these results in a figure using a bar graph or pie chart. Visually displaying results in this way often makes it easier to highlight the results of the survey.

• Finally, with interval scales one could describe the data in terms of *central tendency*. As mentioned earlier, attitude scales are often treated as interval scales so that the central tendency of Likert-scale questions is sometimes calculated. The most common types of central tendency are the mean, mode, and median. The *mean* or average is calculated by adding up the scores and dividing by the number of participants. The *median* is the number in a set of numbers that represents the point at which 50% of the items are above and 50% are below. The *mode* is simply the most common number.

Let's look at how the average or mean could be used to summarize the results of a questionnaire. Assume that you asked students to respond to the question, "Listening is the most important skill for me to develop in English" on a four-point Likert-scale (e.g., Strongly agree = 1, Agree = 2, Disagree = 3, Strongly disagree = 4) and you got from 100 students the following total responses for each item.

1	2	3	4
(Strongly Agree)	(Agree)	(Disagree)	(Strongly Disagree)
52	32	16	0

You also asked students to respond to the question, "Writing is the most important skill for me to develop in English" and received the following responses.

1	2	3	4
(Strongly Agree)	(Agree)	(Disagree)	(Strongly Disagree)
5	10	83	2

You could simply display the data in this manner but you could also compute the difference in the average score of these figures, which would more clearly summarize the differences in the response to these questions. In order to do this, for the first question, you would get the average by multiplying the value of each response by the number of students, resulting in the following:

$$1 \times 52 = 52$$
$$2 \times 32 = 64$$
$$3 \times 16 = 48$$
$$4 \times 0 \underline{0}$$
$$164 \text{ divided by } 100 = 1.64$$

On the other hand, the central tendency for the second question would be the following:

$$
\begin{array}{rcl}
1 \times & 5 & = & 5 \\
2 \times & 10 & = & 20 \\
3 \times & 83 & = & 249 \\
4 \times & 2 & = & \underline{8} \\
& & & 282 \text{ divided by } 100 = 2.8
\end{array}
$$

These measures of central tendency, however, do have not meaning unless the extent of the dispersion around the mean is known. In the example shown above, a mean of 2 could be achieved by all the individuals in the group selecting number 2 (agree). This result is quite different from their being a range of answers from 1 through 4 that result in an average of 2. One way to compute the dispersion of scores around the mean is to compute the standard deviation. The standard deviation is more or less an average of the distance of all the answers from the mean. There is a formula for computing the standard deviation that can be found in all statistic texts. For our purpose, it is important to remember that if researchers are going to display their results using measures of central tendency, they should report the standard deviation. Researchers who use large samples should also include the t-score, which is an indication of the significance of the difference between two means. This determines if the differences found could be due to chance or if they represent a true difference between the means that are being compared. Again, there is a formula for computing the t-score that can be found in statistics texts.

These various ways of displaying data, by number, by percentages, and by average are illustrated in the following data analysis in Fukuda (2003a). In this study Fukuda examined Japanese high school students' and teachers' attitudes toward the treatment of errors in oral communication classes. In her study she distributed questionnaires to 1,085 Japanese high school students and 40 English teachers. One of the questions she asked was the following:

For students:

How often do you want your teachers to treat your spoken errors?

Always	Usually	Sometimes	Occasionally	Never
(100%)	(80%)	(50%)	(20%)	(0%)

For teachers:

How often do you treat your students' spoken errors?

Always	Usually	Sometimes	Occasionally	Never
(100%)	(80%)	(50%)	(20%)	(0%)

TABLE 2.1
Students' and Teachers' Opinions About
the Frequency of Error Treatment

		Always (100%)	Usually (80%)	Sometimes (50%)	Occasionally (20%)	Never (0%)	
		1	2	3	4	5	Mean
Students	Number	259	472	286	60	8	2.16
	Percent	23.9%	43.5%	26.4%	5.5%	0.7%	
Teachers	Number	0	12	14	13	1	3.07
	Percent	0.0%	30.0%	35.0%	32.5%	2.5%	

Source: Fukuda, 2003b, np.

Table 2.1 shows the responses she received on these items. The table summarizes how many respondents selected *always, usually, sometimes, occasionally*, and *never* in answer to the questions listed earlier. The table also includes the percentage of respondents for each response and finally the mean for the question. As discussed earlier, in reporting survey data using the mean, researchers also need to include the standard deviation and *t*-score for the data if the sample size is large, as was the case in Fukuda (2003a).

Open-Ended Questions.   In compiling the results of open-ended questions, you should begin by transcribing the answers. Like the coding of close-ended questions, this is a tedious process. In transcribing the answers, it is best to transcribe the responses as they appear on the survey, with spelling and grammatical problems. If later you decide to modify these responses, this can be done, if it is made clear that changes in grammar and spelling have been made. In categorizing the responses, it is good to anticipate how you might use the data. If you intend to compare the responses on some particular basis such as by gender, ethnic background, or language proficiency, it is a good idea to initially separate the responses according to these categories. If you transcribe the responses on a computer word processing program rather than by hand, it will be much easier to search for particular words or phrases in the data and to move the data around.

   In analyzing the responses, it is helpful to begin by reading over all of the responses and highlighting key ideas that are expressed. Then go over the data several more times to look for reoccurring themes. Use these reoccurring themes to summarize the data that is included in the responses. For each major theme, select one or two typical responses that characterize most of the response that are given. Be certain not to include only clever, unusual, or well-written responses. Remember your purpose is to try to summarize the typical kinds of responses that were given. This whole process can seem very disorganized. As Brown (2001) points out,

> In short, don't be surprised if your research, especially in the data-gathering and compiling stages, is somewhat messy and confusing. When you do your analyses. you will begin to focus on finding patterns of useful information, which will in turn help you to see a clearer picture of what may be going on in your data. (p. 101)

Summarizing Findings. In giving an overall summary of the findings of both the close-ended questions and the open-ended questions, be certain not to over-generalize your findings. General claims can only be made on the basis of large-scale surveys, which are based on a random sample in which inferential statistics have been used to verify that the results of the survey are not due to chance. Because most classroom research will not involve these large samples, it is important to make your conclusions specific to the population that was studied. Hence, if you surveyed the students enrolled in a particular language institute, it is good to preface your conclusions with phrases such as "The students at this language institute appear to favor. . . ."

*   *   *

Exploring the Ideas, 2.3

Listed next is a copy of the survey form that Fukuda (2003a) distributed to more than 1,000 Japanese high school students to get their opinions on the treatment of spoken errors in oral communication classes. Using the criteria contained in the chapter for designing a survey, evaluate Fukuda's survey instrument in terms of the sequencing of the items, the wording of questions, and the general layout.

Questionnaire for Students

Data collected from this anonymous survey will be used for completion of a master's degree in Teaching English to Speakers of Other Language at San Francisco State University. The information gathered will be used for research on error treatment in oral communication classes in Japanese high schools. The purpose of this study is to investigate methods of spoken error treatment and to provide guidelines on how to treat the errors. There are no risks or benefits to you from participating in this research. If you do not wish to participate, you may simply return the blank survey or stop at anytime, with no penalty to yourself. If you do choose to participate, **completion and return of the survey indicates your consent to participate in this study.**

Please do not put your name on this form. The survey should take approximately five minutes to complete. Any questions or concerns should be directed to the principal investigator, Yuko Fukuda, at labchan2@hotmail.com.

Error treatment

I. I want my spoken errors to be treated. Please completely shade in the appropriate letter on your card with pencil. Make sure to only mark one.

	Strongly agree	Agree	Neutral	Disagree	Strongly disagree
1	A	B	C	D	E

II. How often do you want your teachers to treat your spoken errors? Please completely shade in the appropriate letter on your card with pencil. Make sure to only mark one.

	Always (100%)	Usually (80%)	Sometimes (50%)	Occasionally (20%)	Never (0%)
2	A	B	C	D	E

III. When do you want your spoken errors to be corrected? Please completely shade in the appropriate letter on your card with pencil. Make sure to only mark one.

		Strongly agree	Agree	Neutral	Disagree	Strongly disagree
3	As soon as errors are made even if cutting into my speaking	A	B	C	D	E
4	After I speak	A	B	C	D	E
5	After communicative activities	A	B	C	D	E
6	After that day's lesson	A	B	C	D	E

IV. How often do you want each of the following types of errors to be treated? Please completely shade in the appropriate letter on your card with pencil. Make sure to only mark one.

		Always (100%)	Usually (80%)	Sometimes (50%)	Occasionally (20%)	Never (0%)
7	Serious spoken errors that impede a listener's understanding	A	B	C	D	E
8	Less serious spoken errors that do not affect a listener's understanding	A	B	C	D	E
9	Frequent spoken errors	A	B	C	D	E
10	Infrequent spoken errors	A	B	C	D	E
11	Individual errors by only one student	A	B	C	D	E

V. How would you want your teacher to correct your error when you make the following errors? Please completely shade in the appropriate letter on your card with pencil. Make sure to only mark one.

Teacher: Where did you go yesterday?
Student: I _go_ to the park.

	Teachers' error treatment	Very effective	Effective	Neutral	Ineffective	Very ineffective
12	Could you say it again? (Clarification request: The teacher asks the student again.)	A	B	C	D	E
13	I _go_? (Repetition: The teacher highlights the students' grammatical errors by using intonation.)	A	B	C	D	E
14	I went there yesterday, too. (Implicit treatment: The teacher does not interrupt the student but indirectly treats the student's error.)	A	B	C	D	E

15	*Go* is in the present tense. You need to use the past tense *went* here. (Explicit treatment: The teacher gives the correct form to students with grammatical explanation.)	A	B	C	D	E
16	You went yesterday? (Confirmation check: The teacher confirms the student's utterance by giving a correct form.)	A	B	C	D	E
17	Yesterday, I . . . (Elicitation: The teacher elicits the correct form from the student.)	A	B	C	D	E
18	Really? What did you do there? (No correction: The teacher does not treat student's error.)	A	B	C	D	E
19	How does the verb change when we talk about the past? (Metalinguistic feedback: The teacher gives a hint or clue without specifically pointing out the mistake.)	A	B	C	D	E
20	I went to the park. (Recast: The teacher reformulates all or part of student's utterance.)	A	B	C	D	E

VI. I want my spoken errors to be corrected by the following person. Please completely shade in the appropriate letter on your card with pencil. Make sure to only mark one.

		Strongly agree	Agree	Neutral	Disagree	Strongly disagree
21	Japanese speaking teachers	A	B	C	D	E
22	Native English speaking teachers	A	B	C	D	E
23	Classmates	A	B	C	D	E
24	Myself	A	B	C	D	E

Demographics

Please completely shade in the appropriate letter on your card with pencil. Make sure to only mark one.

25. Gender
    A: Male   B: Female
26. What kind of high school are you in?
    A: Public high school   B: Private high school
27. Student's level
    A: First year (freshman)   B: Second year (junior)
    C: Third year (senior)
28. Your first language
    A: Japanese   B: English   C: Others
29. How long have you been studying English?
    A: 0–2 years   B: 2.1–4 years   C: 4.1–6 years   D: 6.1–8 years
    E: More than 8 years
30. Have you studied in any English speaking countries (e.g. USA, UK, Australia, etc.)?
    A: Yes   B: No
31. IF YES, in which country did you study? If more than one, pick the one in which you studied for the longest period of time.
    A: USA   B: UK   C: Australia   D: New Zealand   E: Others

*Thank you for your cooperation. I greatly appreciate it.

Yuko Fukuda
San Francisco State University

* * *

Exploring the Ideas, 2.4

Describe the purpose of a survey you would like to design. In addition, describe the population you would give the survey to. Then write the opening statement you would put on the survey, similar to the one show in *Exploring the Ideas, 2.3*. Finally, draft five to ten items you might use on the survey itself.

* * *

Interviews

Purposes of Interviews

Like surveys, the questions included in an interview can serve different purposes. The purpose of some questions is to find out more about teachers' and students' *background* such as students' knowledge of other languages or teachers' number of years of service. Interview questions can also be designed to find out more about teachers' and learners' *reported behavior* in which researchers ask, for example, about where and with whom students use English or what strategies teachers use to correct student errors. Answers to such questions, of course, indicate only what participants say they do which, given the role relationship that exists in many interview contexts, may reflect more what the interviewees think they should say rather than what they actually do. Finally, questions can be designed to find out more about teachers' and learners' *opinions and attitudes* about various aspects of language learning, such as their feelings about the use of particular classroom activities or the content of classroom materials.

Types of Interviews

Patton (1990) delineates three main types of interviews: (a) the informal conversational interview; (b) the general interview guide approach; and (c) the standardized open-ended interview.

In *informal conversational interviews* generally (a) different questions are asked for each person being interviewed; (b) the same person is interviewed on several occasions; and (c) the length of the interview is completely open ended. Conversation is not being used here in the general sense of informal interactions that have no particular agenda because these conversations do have a purpose; however, in comparison to other types of interviews these interviews are very unstructured. As Patton points out, the strength of an informal conversational interview is that the interviewer can be very responsive to individual respondents and deal with topics as they arise in the conversation. The disadvantage is that a good deal of time is required to collect systematic information. Also because different questions will generate different answers, it is more difficult to find patterns in the data gathered.

When might this type of interview be used in second language research? One context where it is valuable is when researchers want to conduct an intensive case study of one or more teachers or students. For example, if researchers want to find out why particular students are having a great deal of difficulty in class, they might undertake a series of interviews with these students over the course of the semester to find out what linguistic factors and nonlinguistic factors are contributing to the learners' difficulty in acquiring English.

In an *interview guide approach* the interviewer designs a series of questions to ask each participant in order to make certain that the same topics are covered with everyone. Although the order in which these questions are asked and the phrasing of the questions can differ, the same information is asked of everyone. The advantage of this approach is that the same content is covered with each participant, which makes it easier to compile the data. The disadvantage is that the interviewer does not pursue topics that develop from the answers that participants give to particular questions.

The *standardized open-ended interview* is highly structured because the exact wording and order of the questions are specified. Although this type of interview provides no flexibility in the format of the interview, it does assure that all the respondents are asked identical questions. Because of this, all of the data gathered are comparable and the data analysis process easier. A more structured interview is valuable if researchers want to find out particular information from all of the students so that they have a basis on which to compare the students' language learning experience.

In addition to conducting one-on-one interviews, it is possible to have *focus group interviews.* Typically such interviews involve six to eight participants with similar background who are asked to respond to a series of questions. During the interview, teachers and students get to hear what others have to say on a topic and to offer their own views. The gathering is not an open discussion or a problem-solving session; it is instead an interview in which teachers and students are asked a series of prespecified questions. The advantage of holding such sessions is that they can provide a good deal of information in a short time. In addition, the teachers and students involved in the session may appreciate having the opportunity to share their views on particular topics. The disadvantage, however, is that each teacher or student has less opportunity to offer his or her opinion. Additionally, it is difficult to know if a respondent is led to answer in a certain way in order to fit into the group. The primary danger in conducing such sessions is that one or more participants will dominate the interview. This problem can be alleviated if the interviewer manages the interview and encourages everyone to contribute to the discussion.

Conducting Interviews

Wording of Questions.   The success of an interview is related to the wording of the questions. Patton (1990) offers several suggestions in this area. To begin, he urges interviewers to ask truly open-ended questions that allow the participants to respond on their own terms. For example, if a teacher is asked, "How satisfied are you with this textbook?" the response will be phrased in terms of satisfaction. However, if the question is phrased as "What do you think of the textbook?" the teacher can discuss any aspect of the book that he or she believes is important. Patton also warns against using yes/no questions because they do not allow participants to elaborate on their response. Also it is best to avoid questions that deal with more than one idea, such as "What do you think of the program, and how would you improve it?" Finally, with language learners it is important to phrase the questions at a linguistic level that the students can process and to be sensitive to cultural differences.

One way to avoid the problems that can arise from students' lack of English proficiency is, if possible, to allow students to be interviewed in their first language. Kamhi-Stein (2003), for example, in her study of bilingual students' attitudes toward their home language and their beliefs about reading, allowed students to be interviewed in either English or Spanish. Listed here is her interview protocol. Notice that her questions exemplify many of Patton's suggestions. The interview protocol, however, does contain many yes/no questions, which need prompts to elicit additional comments. Her protocol exemplifies a standardized open-ended interview previously described. This format allowed Kamhi-Stein to gather the same data from all of the students regarding their attitudes and beliefs.

Would you like to be interviewed in English or Spanish?

1. How did you learn English?
2. What does the word "reading" mean to you?
3. What are the characteristics of good and poor readers? What are the differences between good and poor readers? Are you a good reader in Spanish? Are you a good reader in English? Please explain.
4. What are the characteristics of a reader who has learned ESL and of a reader who is a native English speaker? Are there any differences between the two?
5. What does a person need to know to be a good English reader? To be a good Spanish reader? Is there a difference?
6. Does being able to read in English help you to read in Spanish? Explain.
7. Does being able to read in Spanish help you to read in English? How?
8. Does being bilingual help you or hurt you when you read? Please explain.
9. Is reading English different from reading Spanish? If so, how?
10. Why do you read?
11. What kind of materials do you read in Spanish? And in English?
12. Do you ever translate from English into Spanish when reading English? If so, please describe what you do?
13. Do you ever translate from Spanish into English when reading Spanish? If so, please describe what you do. (p. 70)

* * *

Exploring the Ideas, 2.5

Listed next are the interview questions that Bellello (2003) used in interviewing her students in order to find out more about their writing habits. Using the criteria previously listed on interview questions, evaluate these questions in terms of their wording and sequencing and make any revisions you believe would improve the interview guide sheet.

1. Tell me what you do when you have a writing assignment. Do you sit down and write? Or do you plan ahead, do you make an outline? Or a cluster of ideas? Give me all the details that you go through when you have a writing assignment.
2. While writing, do you think about vocabulary and grammar? Or do you save it for the end to check or correct? Does thinking about grammar interfere with your writing?
3. When you can't think of the correct word to use when writing, do you stop to look it up, or do you write in your native language and look it up later? Do you think this interferes with your writing process?
4. When you write, how many times do you write or re-write a paragraph, or the whole paper? Once, twice, or more? Do you write a first draft, or several drafts?
5. While writing, do you re-read what you've just written? How often? Never? Seldom, Often, Always?
6. When you write, do you think about who will be reading your paper, or do you just write in order to finish the assignment?
7. What are your greatest challenges or frustrations when writing?
8. Have you had a writing class before? Either in English or your native language? How long was the course? One week, one semester, a year?

* * *

Power Relationships

One of the most problematic aspects of teachers' conducting interviews with their students arises from the fact that teachers are in positions of power. As Nunan (1992) points out, one of the inherent biases of interviews is

> the asymmetrical relationship between the participants. In other words, the participants do not have the same rights, and even in an unstructured relationship, the interviewer has more power than the interviewee. The inequitable relationship between the interviewer and interviewee will affect the content of the interview as well as the language which is used. (p. 150)

How can researchers minimize this bias? One way is for researchers to begin the interview by fully explaining to students why they are conducting the interview, what will be done with the information, and what the benefits are for the student. Another way is to be sensitive to the students' responses, noting when students are having difficulty responding to a question because of a lack of language proficiency, nervousness, or cultural factors, Often it is helpful to recognize these problems and try to reduce the tension that arises from them. Finally, researchers can provide feedback and reinforcement throughout the interview, offering students words of thanks, praise, and support.

No matter how sensitive researchers are to the students they interview, the effect of the power relationship inherent in the interview should not be minimized. What students actually say may, to large extent, be influenced by what they believe is appropriate or desirable to say, given the role relationship that exists between students and teachers. Because all interviews represent a social interaction, Block (2000) contends that researchers should recognize the respective roles of interviewers and interviewees in the interpretation of interview data and not necessarily assume that what an interviewee says reflects reality. Citing Kvale's (1996) work, Block distinguishes two ways to read interview data. One is the *vertical reading* in which what participants say during an interview is seen as reliable. The second type of reading is what Kvale terms a *symptomatic reading* in which what is said in an interview is more about the participants' relationship to the topic being discussed and the social context of the interview than to the topic itself. For example, what is said during a teacher-conducted interview on grades may be largely a factor of the relationship between teachers and students because students may believe that what they say will affect their grades.

Although researchers need to be sensitive to the power relationship in an interview, at the same time it is important to provide a clear direction to the interview. Because interviewers want to use their time effectively, they need to carefully monitor the emphasis that is given to each question. Patton (1990) argues that maintaining control in an interview depends on "(1) knowing what one wants to find out, (2) asking the right questions to get the desired answers, and (3) giving appropriate verbal and nonverbal feedback to the person being interviewed" (p. 330). Attaining these objectives depends on the researcher carefully defining their research objectives and consistently being sensitive to the dynamics of the interview.

Recording Interviews

There are two ways of recording the contents of an interview: tape-recording and note-taking. The advantage of *tape-recording* an interview is that this preserves the actual language that is used, providing an objective record of what was said that can later be analyzed. The disadvantage is that the presence of a tape recorder can add to the anxiety of the participants. Additionally, transcribing the recording can be quite tedious and result in a great deal of data, some of which may not be valuable. If you choose to use a tape recorder be certain to check the equipment before the interview and take along extra tapes. When you start the interview, place the microphone in a central location and check the recording system. After the interview is over, listen to the tape and take notes on important sections of the interview.

Note-taking allows a researcher to record the central facts and issues in an interview. It is also far easier to analyze the data summarized in notes than what is provided in a transcript. The disadvantage, of course, is that a researcher does not have an objective word-for-word record of what was said. In addition, taking notes while listening is extremely difficult and trying to do so can reduce the rapport of the interview. There are several benefits of taking very abbreviated notes even if the session is being tape-recorded. First, these notes can remind you of the topics that have been covered and help you formulate additional questions. Second, having notes will facilitate your analysis of the transcripts by highlighting important parts of the interview. Finally, taking notes can serve as a nonverbal cue, signaling to the interviewee when something important has been said. The notes themselves should consist primarily of key phrases and major points in the interview. It is also useful to write summary notes immediately after the interview is over when specific information from the interview can be recalled.

Analyzing Interview Data

The analysis of interview data should begin during the interview process itself. As you conduct interviews look for key ideas that may provide the basis for data analysis. However, be certain not to allow your initial interpretations to distort your additional data collection. Rather try to keep an open mind and look for alternative explanations and patterns in the data. Also as you gather your interview data, be certain to make an additional copy of your transcripts or notes and to keep them in a safe place. Finally, label all of your interview data by the person interviewed, the date of the interview, and the page of the field notes or transcript.

Case Versus Cross-Case Analysis. As Patton (1990) points out, the first decision that needs to be made in analyzing interview data is to decide whether to begin with a case analysis or a cross-case analysis. Using a *case analysis* means writing a case study for each person that was interviewed. This approach would be appropriate if you wish to highlight the individuals involved in your study and the manner in which they differ. For example, if you are doing a case study of three students who have consistently performed poorly in class, you may want to highlight the manner in which their poor performance stems from different sources. The second major way to organize the data is to use a *cross-case analysis*, which involves organizing the responses of several interviewees according to the topics raised in the interviews. This is fairly easy to do if you have used a standardized open-ended interview. This approach would be appropriate if you wish to highlight particular aspects of your research topic. For example, if you interviewed a variety of teachers on their opinions regarding the use of group work and asked questions regarding the advantages and disadvantages of using group work, these topics could provide the organizational framework for the data analysis. It is, of course, possible to combine these two approaches.

Content Analysis.   Once you have gathered all of your interview data, you can begin your content analysis in detail. This involves identifying and coding key topics in your data. One way to begin is to read the data over a variety of times, looking for key ideas or topics and labeling these ideas by marginal notes or post-its. If your data is computerized you can also employ some type of computer software to help you analyze the data. Two popular software programs for analyzing qualitative data are QSR NUD*IST (Qualitative Solutions and Research Pty., 1995) and its partner product QSR NVivo. No matter what method you select, however, your overall goal is to arrive at a list of categories that develop from the data and capture the ideas in the data. Once you have arrived at a list of these categories, you can then return to the data and code the data according to these categories. The study by Borg (1998) provides a clear model of how this process can be undertaken.

Borg (1998) was interested in finding out on what basis teachers make pedagogical decisions in the teaching of grammar. In his study he examined how one experienced EFL teacher approached grammar teaching in his classroom. He began with a pre-observation interview in which he asked the teacher questions about his own education, his entry into the profession and his development as a teacher, his reflections on teaching, and the school where he taught. He then observed the teacher in his classroom for 15 hours over a period of 2 weeks. After each class he looked for key instructional episodes that might generate questions about the teacher's approach to the teaching of grammar. These episodes included such items as the teacher's use of a particular grammar activity, the explanation of a grammar rule, or the teacher's correction of a student's grammatical error. Borg then selected various key episodes and interviewed the teacher to find out what he was trying to do at a particular stage in the lesson and why he acted the way he did. The interviews with the teacher were all transcribed and then analyzed to determine key factors in this teacher's approach to grammar teaching.

Borg used a variety of manual and computerized strategies to code the data. He initially analyzed his data according to a *start list* (Miles & Huberman, 1994) of conceptual categories that were derived from his interview data. Data that didn't fit into these categories led Borg to generate additional categories that would cover all of the data. This process led Borg to eventually analyze the interview data into three central categories: experiential factors (i.e., references to the teacher's educational and professional experiences), pedagogical factors (i.e., the teacher's beliefs about L2 teaching and learning) and contextual factors (i.e., references the teacher made to external contextual factors like time and internal factors like the student's age and proficiency level).

Borg's (1998) analysis of his interview data illustrates how researchers need to develop categories from the data by returning to the data over and over again, looking for patterns, and modifying existing categories to accommodate new insights. In reporting on his study, Borg used his analysis of the data to support his interpretations of the classroom episodes he observed. He included representative examples from the interview data to demonstrate his interpretations of the target teacher's approach to teaching grammar.

* * *

Exploring the Ideas, 2.6

Describe a study you would like to undertake that involves interviewing a group of students or teachers using a standardized open-ended interview. In your summary describe

- the purpose of the study;
- the theoretically-driven list of topics you want to cover in the interview; and
- the group of teachers or students you would interview.

Then write five to ten questions you would use in the interview.

Your study, for example, could involve interviewing students regarding their attitudes toward the use of peer review in writing classes. After consulting the literature on this topic, you should develop a list of topics or concerns addressed in other studies on students' attitudes toward peer review. Then using this list of topics, write five to ten interview questions you would use.

* * *

Exploring the Ideas, 2.7

Read one of the survey research studies listed below and then answer the questions that follow. If you are familiar with another survey research report, you can analyze this article instead.

Articles

Bardovi-Harlig, & Dornyei, Z. (1998). Do language learners recognize pragmatic violations? Pragmatic versus grammatical awareness in instructed L2 learning. *TESOL Quarterly, 32*(2), 233–262. (This study used a Likert-scale to determine students' assessment of the seriousness of grammatical and pragmatic errors.)

Li, D. (1998). "It's always more difficult than you plan and imagine": Teachers' perceived difficulties in introducing the communicative approach in South Korea. *TESOL Quarterly, 32*(4), 677–703. (This study used a written survey and interview questions to determine South Korean secondary school teachers' perceived difficulties in using a communicative approach.)

Mangelsdorf, K. (1992). Peer review in the ESL composition classroom: What do the students think. *ELT Journal, 46*(3), 274–284. (Mangelsdorf used open-ended written questions to determine ESL students' opinion of the use of peer review in their writing class.)

Questions

1. What is the research question?
2. Where was the survey/interview conducted?
3. What was the population surveyed? What sampling procedures were used?
4. How were the data collected?
5. Were the questions used in the survey or interview well-designed in terms of the standards discussed in the chapter?
6. How were the data analyzed? If open-ended questions were used, does the researcher describe how they were analyzed and coded?
7. How were the data presented? If the study includes numerical data, how were they reported—by frequency, percentage, and/or mean? If the mean is reported, is the standard deviation reported?
8. What conclusions were drawn? Are they justified in light of the data presented?
9. What are the pedagogical implications of the study? Are they warranted in light of the findings of the study?

*   *   *

INTROSPECTIVE RESEARCH

Verbal Reports

Defining Verbal Reports

There is widespread agreement that it is important to know more about how successful and unsuccessful learners' process a second language. The primary problem in finding out more about these cognitive processes is designing a method for studying thought processes. One of the few available means for doing this is verbal reports or verbal protocols, first used by Newell and Simon (1972). Verbal reports "are oral records of thoughts, provided by subjects when thinking aloud during or immediately after completing a task" (Kasper, 1998, p. 358).

There are two kinds of verbal reports. The first, *a think-aloud*, asks learners to verbalize their thought processes while they are involved in processing language, typically reading a text or writing an essay. The second type is *a retrospective report* in which learners verbalize their thought processes immediately after they process the language. Retrospective reports can be used with listening and speaking tasks or after a think-aloud to explore some of the comments made by students during the think-aloud. It is important to recognize that verbal protocols do not mirror the thought process. As Kasper (1998) puts it,

> Verbal protocols are not immediate revelations of thought processes. They represent (a subset of) the information currently available in short-term memory rather than the processes producing the information. Cognitive processes are not directly manifest in protocols but have to be inferred, just as in the case of other types of data. (p. 358)

Many criticisms have been leveled against verbal reports, the major one being that it is highly unnatural and obtrusive to verbalize one's thoughts. In addition, as Kasper noted, verbal reports do not elicit all of the cognitive processes involved in an activity and thus are incomplete. Furthermore, the analysis of verbal report data is subject to the idiosyncratic interpretations of the researcher and hence may not be valid. For second language learners there is also the problem that students are asked to report on their thought processes in a second language. Although few dispute the limitations of verbal reports, at this point, the method is one of the few available means for finding out more about the thought processes of second language learners.

Conducting Verbal Reports

Brown and Rodgers (2002) list several principles that should be adhered to in conducing verbal reports. These principles include the following:

1. time intervening between mental operations and report is critical and should be minimized as much as possible;
2. verbalization places additional cognitive demands on mental processing that requires care in order to achieve insightful results;
3. verbal reports of mental processes should avoid the usual social conventions of talking to someone;
4. there is a lot of information in introspective reports aside from the words themselves. Researchers need to be aware of these parallel signal systems and be prepared to include them in their analyses;
5. verbal reports of automatic processes are not possible. Such processes include visual and motor processes and low-attention, automatized linguistic processes such as the social chat of native speakers. (p. 55)

The first principle suggests that students' verbal reports should occur either while the activity is occurring or as soon as possible afterward. Principle two is especially significant for researchers conducting verbal reports with L2 speakers. It suggests that, if possible, students should be allowed to use their first language, if this reduces the cognitive demands of the process. Principle three, four, and five suggest that the role of the researcher should be as unobtrusive as possible, that the researcher should take note of the nonverbal behavior as well as the verbal behavior of the student, and that verbal reports cannot be used to report automatic thought processes.

The following are some procedures to follow in conducting verbal reports.

• To begin, *provide students with a practice activity* to get them familiar with verbal reports. You might begin by having them do a simple multiplication task and ask them to think aloud as they do so. You can also have them do a task similar to the one they are going to do. For example, if they are going to do a think-aloud on a reading text, you might give them a short reading passage for practice. You can also begin the session by modeling a think-aloud for them as you read a passage.

• *Give simple directions.* Basically you need to tell the students to verbalize everything they are thinking as they complete a task. They should imagine that they are talking to themselves about what they are thinking.

You should also point out that occasionally you may be reminding them to think out loud.

• During the think-aloud, *be as unobtrusive as possible.* This means that after you acquaint students with the process and give them directions, you should recede into the background as much as possible, speaking only when the student lapses into silence by giving a gentle reminder, such as "Remember to think aloud." Because you want students to focus on reporting on their cognitive processes and not talk to you, it is helpful to sit behind the students so as to discourage them from talking to you.

• If students are doing a think-aloud on a reading text, you might *ask students to report their thought processes at particular points* in the text after they have read the passage. This can be done by having students read the text out aloud. Then place a signal at specific points in the passage where you want them to stop and talk about what they are thinking.

• When you are prompting students to think aloud, be certain to simply remind them to verbalize what they are thinking and *don't ask leading questions.* The use of leading questions can be a particular problem in conducting retrospective reports when you are encouraging students to report on the thoughts they just had while they were completing the activity. For example, if you are using a listening task, when you stop the tape, you should ask students to tell you what they are thinking or ask what they think is going on and not ask questions like "Did you find the tape confusing?"

• Whether you are conducting a think-aloud or a retrospective report, it is essential that you *record the session* because this data will provide the basis for your analysis. As with an interview, it is important to check your equipment before you begin the session and to put the microphone in a central position.

• Because nonverbal behavior can often signal cognitive processes, *pay attention to students' nonverbal behavior* as they complete the task, as, for example, if they stop writing during a writing task. Ideally it is best to videotape the session so that you can capture the nonverbal behavior. However, using a video-camera can be distracting for the students.

Analyzing the Data

The first step in analyzing a verbal report is to transcribe the data and then segment the transcript into thought units. Each thought unit is then coded according to the function that it serves. The most difficult part of verbal report studies is coding the thought units because the coding system needs to be comprehensive enough to include all of the data. Arriving at a unique coding system is a very time consuming and tedious process. In order to make the process simpler, it is essential to begin by reviewing the coding systems that presently exist in the literature. By reviewing these coding systems you may find one that is quite suitable for your data, or you can combine several existing coding systems to fit your own data.

In coding verbal report data, you should get a second rater to code your data and then determine the degree of inter-rater reliability. If this is not possible, you should try to code the data at two different times to determine your own intra-rater reliability. This is necessary because very often categories overlap so that some examples can easily be placed in more than one category. By having a second reader for your data and discussing differences in your coding, you can arrive at more precise definitions of particular categories.

Verbal Report Research

Block (1986) used think-aloud protocols with 6 nonnative speakers of English (3 native speakers of Spanish and 3 native speakers of Chinese) and 3 native speakers of English, all college freshmen enrolled in a remedial reading course. The students read two passages taken from a textbook used in an introductory psychology course that most students took. After the students completed the think-alouds, Block transcribed the think-alouds, segmented them into thought units, and then categorized the thought units into the categories listed below. She then compared how often each of the students used specific strategies in order to characterize the reading processes of each student.

Block delineated two general modes in the thought processes these students engaged in as they read these passages. The first mode was what she termed the *reflexive mode* in which students related affectively and personally to the text, directing their attention away from the text. The second was what she was termed an *extensive mode* in which students attempted to deal with the message conveyed by the author. Block also categorized all of the students' responses according to strategy type. The strategies were of two types—*general strategies* that included comprehension-gathering and comprehension-monitoring strategies and *local strategies* that dealt with attempts to understand specific linguistic units. The following is her description of the general strategy categories.

1. *Anticipate content:* The reader predicts what content will occur in succeeding portions of the text. This strategy can occur in either mode but occurred more frequently in the extensive mode. "I guess the story will be about how you go about talking to babies."

2. *Recognize text structure:* The reader distinguishes between the main points and supporting details or discusses the purpose of information. Responses occurred in the extensive mode. "This is an example of what baby talk is."

3. *Integrate information:* The reader connects new information with previously stated content. Responses occurred in the extensive mode. "Oh, this connects with the sentence just before."

4. *Question information in the text:* The reader questions the significance or veracity of content. Responses were in the extensive mode. "Why is [baby talk among adults] usually limited to lovers?"

5. *Interpret the text:* The reader makes an inference, draws a conclusion, or forms a hypothesis about the content. Responses, though more frequent in the extensive mode, did occur in the reflexive mode, such as, "I think that's why some people doing this."

6. *Use general knowledge and associations:* The readers in this study used their knowledge and experience (a) to explain, extend, and clarify content; (b) to evaluate the veracity of content; and (c) to react to content. Responses were frequently in the reflexive mode: "When they talk to a baby, they just sing little songs which brought to mind again my little nephew because when he hears sounds he just open his eyes and he looks and he'll try to clap and sing with them." However, some readers used information from their own lives to clarify or extend ideas in the passages, and these responses were considered to be in the extensive mode. "That's true. It's not easy to hold baby's attention."

7. *Comment on behavior or process:* The reader describes strategy use, indicates awareness of the components of the process, or expresses a sense of accomplishment or frustration. Because readers' responses reflect self-awareness, this strategy was not classified by mode. "I'm getting this feeling I always get when I read like I lost a word."

8. *Monitor comprehension:* The reader assesses his or her degree of understanding of the text. This strategy occurred in the extensive mode. "Now I see what it means." "It doesn't seem like what I'm thinking of."

9. *Correct behavior:* The reader notices that an assumption, interpretation, or paraphrase is incorrect and changes that statement. This is a combination of the strategies of integration and monitoring, since the reader must both connect new information with old and evaluate understanding. This strategy occurred in the extensive mode. "Now I read this part I understand . . . I misunderstood in a way."

10. *React to the text:* The reader reacts emotionally to information in the text. Responses occurred in the reflexive mode. "I love little babies." (pp. 472–473)

If you decide to conduct a think-aloud on a reading text with some of your students, you might begin by using an existing category system like Block's and then modify it to suit your particular data.

* * *

Exploring the Ideas, 2.8

Listed here is a transcript of one of the verbal reports gathered by Minami (in press) in a study of sustained-content reading and its effect on reading comprehension. In the following protocol, the student is doing a think-aloud on a reading selection that appeared in the *New York Times* entitled, "What pop lyrics say to us today." Using the categories on general reading strategies listed in the chapter by Block (1986), try to categorize the comments made by the student in the verbal protocol. To start, segment the verbal protocol into thought units. Then try to categorize each segment according to Block's categories. If possible, share your categorization with other classmates to determine the extent to which you agree on your categorization. When you have differences, explain your rationale for including the segment in one category rather than another.

The following is a possible analysis of the first line. The first thought unit is "Does pop lyrics mean pop singer?" This is an example of category 4, questioning information in the text. The student is questioning the significance of the term *pop lyrics*. The second thought unit is "I don't know." This is an instance of category 8, monitoring comprehension, in which the reader assesses his or her understanding of the text. The third thought unit is "maybe let's see." This is an example of category 1, anticipating content, because the student predicts the text will answer his or her question.

Student C's transcription

(Note: The sections in bold italics are the students' verbal report regarding the preceding section of the reading text.)

What pop lyrics say to us today.

Does pop lyrics mean pop singer? I don't know . . . maybe, let's see.

Appeared in slightly different form in the *New York Times* February 24, 1985. By Robert Palmer.

Ok, so that means "slightly different". They changed it a little in this article. 1985. That's really old article. Robert Palmer. The author is maybe a White. Okay.

Bruce Springsteen became the first rock lyricist to be courted by both of the major candidates in a presidential election last fall.

Ummm (pause) So, Bruce Springsteen . . . is he a rock star? "Courted by" What does this mean? I don't know. I'll continue. Maybe I can figure it out.

First Ronald Reagan singled him out as an artist whose songs instill pride in America. *Ummm, so his songs . . . still very influential in American? It means he's still big?*

Walter Mondale retaliated,

"Retaliated"? I don't know this. "Re" . . . okay, so say something repeat again.

asserting that *he* had won the rock star's endorsement.

Okay, so this guy wanna make . . . uh . . . put emphasis on he had won rock star's endorsement. What is "endorsement"? Is this a price?

"Bruce may have been born to run," Mr. Mondale quipped, quoting the title of a Springsteen hit, "but he wasn't born yesterday."

Ummm, "born to run" . . . what does this mean? (reread) I don't understand this part. Let me read more.

Rock is part of adult culture now, to an extent that would have been unthinkable in the mid-1970s.

What's that? "Rock is a part of adult culture now" Maybe . . . because I feel like rock is culture of . . . that's an expression of youth culture. Never been an adult culture. Maybe because Americans in those days become old now, so rock becomes adult culture. Okay, that can explain why "to an extent that would have been unthinkable in the middle 1970s." Okay so in middle 1970s, everyone think rock'n'roll only kids listen to that. But now most middle-aged men listen to that.

It is no longer the exclusive reserve of young people sending messages to each other.

Okay, the same meaning again.

*   *   *

Exploring the Ideas, 2.9

Read one of the verbal report studies listed below and then answer the questions that follow. If you are familiar with another verbal report research report, you can analyze this article instead.

Verbal Report Studies

Block, E. (1986). The comprehension strategies of second language readers. *TESOL Quarterly, 20*(3), 463–494. (This study reports on the use of think-aloud protocols to examine the reading comprehension strategies of native and nonnative English speakers enrolled in a remedial reading class.)

Gu, Y. (2003). Fine brush and freehand: The vocabulary learning art of two successful Chinese EFL learners. *TESOL Quarterly, 37*(1), 73–104. (This study reports on the use of think-aloud protocols to examine the vocabulary-learning strategies of 2 Chinese learners of English.)

Goh, C. M. (2002). Exploring listening comprehension tactics and their interaction patterns. *System, 30,* 185–206. (This study examines the retrospective reports of 2 students from the People's Republic of China after undertaking listening tasks.)

Questions

1. What is the research question?
2. Where was the verbal report conducted?
3. Who were the participants, and why were they selected?
4. How were the data collected? Did the researcher report on the procedures used for conducting the verbal report?
5. Did the researcher use an existing coding system or design an original coding system? If the researcher devised an original coding system, what procedures did he/she use to develop this coding system?
6. How were the data presented? Does the author include a numerical analysis of the use of particular categories? Does the author use sufficient examples from the data to make the categories clear?
7. What conclusions were drawn from the analysis? Are they justified in light of the data that is included in the article?
8. What are the pedagogical implications of the study? Are they warranted in light of the findings of the study?

* * *

Diary Studies

Defining Diary Studies

The use of diary studies to investigate L2 teaching and learning is a relatively new method. One of the first definitions of diary studies was offered by Bailey and Ochsner (1983):

A diary study in second language learning, acquisition, or teaching is an account of a second language experience as recorded in a first-person journal. The diarist may be a language teacher or a language learner—but the central characteristic of the diary studies is that they are introspective: The diarist studies his own teaching or learning. Thus he can report on affective factors, language learning strategies, and his own perceptions—facets of the language learning experience which are normally hidden or largely inaccessible to an external observer. (p. 189)

According to Bailey (1991), diary studies are essentially first-person case studies in which the research genre is defined by the data collection procedure: "A language learner keeps an intensive journal using introspection and/or retrospection, as well as observation, typically over a period of time. The data analysis may be done by diarist himself or by an independent researcher using the learner's diary (or some 'public' version of that diary) as data" (pp. 60–61). Although many diaries are reported in unpublished manuscripts or theses, some language learning and teaching diaries have been published. One of the most cited language learning diaries is that undertaken by Schmidt and Frota (1986) in which Schmidt, a linguist himself, described his struggles in learning Portuguese. Some language learning diary studies have involved a third person analyzing the diaries of language learners. Bailey (1983), for example, examined eleven diaries of adult L2 learners to investigate the competitiveness and anxiety of these learners.

Strengths and Weaknesses of Diary Studies

Because diary studies are based on introspection, some have questioned the value of such studies. An excellent discussion of the strengths and weaknesses of diary studies is Bailey (1991). In this article Bailey applies the doubting and believing game to diary studies. In the doubting game, one takes a critical stance toward what is being investigated. In reference to diary studies, the following doubts can be raised.

- First, most diary studies involve a small number of learners looking at different aspects of the L2 learning process. Hence, it is difficult to compare the findings of the studies.
- Second, most diary studies published so far have been undertaken by linguists, experienced teachers, or language teachers in training. Because of this, they may not be representative of typical language learners.
- Third, diary studies are based on subjective data, based entirely on the teachers' or learners' perceptions with no other data that allows for verification of the conclusions drawn.
- Finally, one can question the extent to which individuals can analyze all of the processes involved in their own language learning and teaching experiences.

In the believing game, on the other hand, one accepts the assertions of diarist and the idea that all experience is subjective. In applying the believing game to diary studies, Bailey (1991) maintains that for both teachers and learners, keeping a diary can provide a great deal of self-awareness of the processes they are involved in. In addition, Bailey argues that diary studies can provide the following benefits for L2 teaching and learning research.

- First, like other introspective methods, diary studies can provide information about L2 learners and teachers and their perspectives on the affective and instructional factors that affect L2 learning and teaching.
- Second, diary studies allow researchers to see factors identified by teachers and learners that may not be readily identified by researchers as worth studying.
- Third, diary studies when used with other sources of data can provide a vehicle for data triangulation.
- Finally, the data collection process itself is more accessible in that it is " 'low-tech,' portable, and trainable." (p. 88)

Whereas the procedure for diary studies is less complex than some other methods, there are nonetheless particular procedures that need to be followed.

Conducting Diary Studies

A diary study must involve more than just making regular introspective entries regarding L2 learning and teaching. The diary is only the data. In order to be a study, there must be a careful analysis of the data. In conducting a diary study, Bailey (1990) recommends that the following steps be taken.

1. The diarist provides an account of personal language learning or teaching history.
2. The diarist systematically records events, details, and feelings about the current language experience in the diary.
3. The diarist revises the journal entries for the public version of the diary, clarifying meaning in the process.
4. The diarist studies the journal entries, looking for patterns and significant events. (Also, other researchers may analyze the diary entries.)
5. The factors identified as being important to the language learning or teaching experience are interpreted and discussed in the final diary study. Ideas from the pedagogy literature may be added at this stage. (p. 219)

Although Bailey suggests that ideas from the literature not be added until the final stage, researchers may find it valuable to reflect on what they have read in pedagogy literature as they analyze the data, looking for patterns and their significance. Bailey makes some other suggestions regarding the process of undertaking a diary study. She maintains that diary entries must be candid if they are to be of benefit. She also suggests that a teacher set aside a time each day immediately following class to write in the diary and that the time allotted to writing should at least equal the time spent in class. Most importantly, she recommends that diarists consistently ask themselves what evidence they have to support the statements they make and wherever possible support their reflective comments with examples from class sessions or language data. Unfortunately, at this point there are few published L2 learning and teaching diary studies to look to for models and insight. However, as Bailey (1990) notes, those who have written unpublished diary studies consistently point to the benefit of diary studies in promoting their own awareness of the L2 teaching and learning process.

* * *

Exploring the Ideas, 2.10

Read one of the diary studies listed below and then answer the questions that follow. If you are familiar with other diary studies, you can analyze these articles instead.

Diary Studies Report

Bailey, K. M. (1983). Competitiveness and anxiety in adult second language learning: Looking at and through the diary studies. In H. W. Selinger & M. H. Long (Eds.), *Classroom oriented research in second language acquisition* (pp. 67–103). Rowley, MA: Newbury House. (In this study Bailey analyzes the diaries of 10 learners of English to determine how competitiveness and anxiety influenced their language learning.)

Numrich, C. (1996). On becoming a language teacher: Insights from diary studies. *TESOL Quarterly, 30*(1), 131–154. (Numrich analyzes the diaries of 22 novice teachers discussing their practicum experience to delineate their common concerns.)

Schmidt, R. W., & Froda, S. N. (1986). Developing basic conversational ability in a second language: A case study of an adult learner of Portuguese. In R. R. Day (Ed.), *Talking to learn: Conversation in second language acquisition* (pp. 237–326). Rowley, MA: Newbury House. (This study reports on Schmidt's use of a diary to analyze his experiences learning Portuguese.)

Questions

1. What is the research question?
2. Where was the diary study conducted?

3. Who were the participants?
4. How were the data collected?
5. How were the data analyzed?
6. Has the author used convincing and relevant excerpts from the data to support the point he/she wishes to make? If so, provide examples of this data.
7. What conclusions were drawn from the study? Are they justified in light of the data that is included in the article?
8. What are the pedagogical implications of the study? Do they seem warranted in light of the findings of the study?

* * *

QUALITATIVE RESEARCH

Case Studies

Defining Case Studies

Case studies are one of the more difficult methodologies to define because they can vary in focus and research data. In essence, a case study is a single instance of some bound system, which can range from one individual to a class, a school, or an entire community. The data gathered can include interview data, narrative accounts, classroom observations, verbal reports, and written documents. The researcher selects which type of data to gather based on the theoretical orientation that informs the investigation. For example, if a researcher assumes that the success of a particular group of young children in acquiring English depends largely on peer and parental interaction, as well as classroom instruction, then the researcher will include data that document the influence of these factors on learning English. Researchers generally select a case study methodology if they believe that contextual conditions are highly relevant to their research focus.

Hitchcock and Hughes (1995) maintain that a case study has the following distinctive features.

- It is concerned with a rich and vivid description of events relevant to the case.
- It provides a chronological narrative of events relevant to the case.
- It blends a description of events with the analysis of them.
- It focuses on individual actors or groups of actors and seeks to understand their perceptions of events.

- It highlights specific events that are relevant to the case.
- An attempt is made to portray the richness of the case in writing up the report. (p. 317, as cited in Cohen, Manion, & Morrison, 2000, p. 182)

Applying these characteristics to L2 classroom-based research, a researcher using a case study methodology would seek to understand the L2 teaching and learning process from the perspective of the teachers and students being studied. The researcher would also provide a rich description of the many contextual factors that surround the case being investigated.

Yin (2003) argues that case studies can serve a variety of purposes, which include the following.

1. Case studies can *explain the causal links* in real life situations. A case study could, for example, investigate the causes of a particular learner's unwillingness to participate in group work.
2. Case studies can *describe an intervention* and the context in which it occurred. For example, a case study could describe a particular classroom and the intervention that a teacher undertook to alter some dimension of his or her classroom. This type of case study is an action research case study.
3. A case study can *evaluate a particular case.* In such case studies a researcher could, for example, evaluate the implementation of a new curriculum in a particular school.

In the area of L2 teaching and learning, case studies are frequently used to trace the language development of a particular group of learners. These studies are longitudinal studies of one or more learner. Schmidt and Froda's (1986) study of Schmidt learning Portuguese for a 5-month period in Brazil is a case in point. A case study may also be part of a larger study. A school program evaluation, for example, might include case studies of several individual schools. Also a long-term ethnographic study might include several shorter individual cases, as was the case with Peirce's (1995a) work with immigrant women.

Conducting Case Study Research

The design of a case study has several components. Yin (2003) maintains that a case study design must have the following features.

1. *A research question*—In many case studies, this question is in the form of a "how" or "why" question because the design of a case study allows such questions to be addressed.

2. *A proposition*—The proposition typically reflects a theoretical orientation and points the researcher in the direction of where to look for relevant data. For example, if a researcher wants to examine how the input a learner has available influences his or her progress in English, the researcher might examine the interaction this individual has in English in the classroom, the home, and the community.

3. *A unit of analysis*—Central to a case study is defining what the case is. Is it an individual, a group of learners, an intact classroom, a school, or a program? The research question should specify the boundaries of the case. Once the unit of analysis has been defined, then the researcher can read studies on similar cases.

4. *The logic linking the data to the proposition*—Yin suggests that one way to establish links between the data and the proposition of the study is to look for patterns in the data that may support the study's proposition. For example, if a researcher believed that a particular group of students' resistance to group work was due to their cultural background, the researcher might look for evidence in the data gathered that supported this view and evidence that did not support it. Studying the negative evidence could produce a counter proposition. This endeavor of matching evidence to counter propositions is termed *pattern matching*.

5. *The criteria for interpreting the findings*—This component has to do with establishing how much evidence is necessary to warrant a particular interpretation. Hopefully by undertaking pattern matching a researcher will find that one proposition is supported by far more data than an alternative proposition.

As with all sound research, case study researchers must strive for validity and reliability in their investigation. In terms of external validity, one of the major criticisms of case study research is that a single case provides very little evidence for generalizing. Yin (2003) argues that accepting the definition of validity used in experimental research is not warranted because case studies do not claim to be based on a representative sample in which statistical procedures can verify generalizations. He contends that statistical generalizations are valid for empirical research, but case study research depends on analytical generalizations in which the findings of a study can lend support to some broader theory. In regard to reliability, case study researchers, like all researchers, must make certain that if another researcher were to conduct a comparable case study, they would come to similar findings. In order to accomplish this, case study researchers must carefully document all the procedures they follow in as much detail as possible.

One way to increase the reliability of a case study is to have a protocol that guides the researcher in the collection of data. Yin (2003) maintains that *a case study protocol* should have the following sections.

- *An overview of the case study project.* In this section researchers summarize the objectives of the project, the issues being examined, and relevant readings on the issue.
- *Field procedures.* Here researchers explain procedural steps, such as how they will get access to case sites and obtain informed consent forms.
- *Case study questions.* Here researchers define the specific questions they will investigate and describe the data they will gather to answer these questions.
- *A guide for the case study report.* Here the researchers outline how they plan to organize the report and deal with the data.

These components contain many of the features dealt with in chapter 1 in the section on research design. Notice, however, that with a case study, researchers generally begin with some specific research questions. As we shall see shortly, ethnographic research typically has a much less well-defined question in the initial stages of the study.

Case Study Research

One clear example of case study research is Leki (1995). In this study, Leki, as with most qualitative research, began with a general research question. She was concerned with how ESL students acquire the writing forms needed for their academic discipline and how their experience in their non-ESL courses helped to shape their acquisition of these forms. Also in the tradition of qualitative research, she gathered a variety of data including interview notes, student journals, classroom observations, and all of the students' written materials. However, unlike ethnographic studies, the study was completed in only one semester. Finally, in the tradition of most case studies, Leki focused on only 5 target students.

As a way to aid you in reading published reports critically, we examine the Leki article more closely, focusing on questions outlined by Johnson (1992, p. 91) for analyzing case studies.

1. What is the research question?
The study does not list an explicit research question but rather in the introduction states that the study focuses on examining how 5 ESL students cope with the academic writing demands they have in their classes across the curriculum during their first semester of study.

2. In what context was the research conducted?
The study was conducted at a large state university in the U.S.

3. Who were the participants in the study? How were they selected? What were their relevant characteristics?

Initially 60 students volunteered to be part of the study. However, Leki chose only students who had had no previous experience with a U.S. educational institution and were enrolled in courses that required a significant amount of writing. She also selected students that represented differences in gender, home country, year in school, and academic subject area. The participants were 3 graduate students and 2 undergraduate students.

4. What was the theoretical orientation of the researcher?

Although the article does not contain a specific section that specifies the theoretical orientation of the study, the introduction sets forth an important assumption that informs the study. Leki contends that students' writing development is not solely a factor of their ESL writing class but rather a factor of their general academic literacy experience, as well as their personal experience. In this way she supports the ideological model of literacy discussed in chapter 1 in which the influence of the social context on writing is highlighted.

5. What was the role of the researcher?

Leki was not a participant of the study because she was not one of the students' instructor. Rather her role was to interview the students, observe their classes, and examine students' written work.

6. What data-collection procedures were used? How much time was spent collecting data?

The study spanned one academic semester. Leki interviewed each of the 5 students once a week for most of the semester. The interviews lasted approximately an hour and were transcribed. At least one professor of each student was interviewed for an hour. Leki also observed their academic writing classes and examined relevant written documents including everything the students wrote for the courses and all the materials that were distributed in the course. In addition, the students kept journals in which they recorded anything that was important to them in relation to their academic experience.

7. How were data analyzed? What were the findings?

Leki used analytic induction in which she repeatedly examined the data she gathered in order to discover some reoccurring patterns. This inductive process led her to delineate various coping strategies that the students used to deal with the academic writing demands they faced. These include such strategies as relying on past writing experiences, looking for models, accommodating teachers' demands, and resisting teachers' demands. By examining how each student used some or all of these strategies, she highlighted how individual students deal with their academic writing demands in different ways.

8. What conclusions are drawn? Are they logically related to the descriptive data?

Leki concludes that the ESL students she studied already came to the university with some very well developed strategies for dealing with their academic writing demands and that, furthermore, they were able to alter these strategies and adopt new ones when necessary. Her conclusions were well supported by the data she gathered from the interviews with the target students.

9. What is the contribution of the study to our knowledge of social or contextual factors in L2 learning?

The study illustrates how students used the strategies they already had to cope with the demands of their writing assignments. The students knew how to draw on what they knew to meet the writing requirements of a specific context.

10. What are the stated implications for teaching?

Leki argues that because the students in her study had well developed writing strategies that they brought with them from their prior writing experiences, instructors in ESL classes should attempt to build on the strategies students already have and not spend time teaching them strategies they already are quite familiar with. She also argues that because writing demands differ across disciplines, ESL teachers need to teach students general strategies that they can adopt to various social contexts.

The Leki study exemplifies all of the features previously listed that Hitchcock and Hughes (1995, cited in Cohen, Manion, & Morrison, 2000) contend a case study should have. The study provides a vivid narrative description of the events related to the students' writing experiences. It blends a description of the events with an analysis of them. By including a section on each student with comments from the interviews, the study seeks to portray the students' perception of their experience. Finally, the article highlights specific examples of students' writing experiences that are relevant to the theoretical assumptions of the study.

*   *   *

Exploring the Ideas, 2.11

Read one of the case studies listed below and then answer the questions for analyzing case studies. If you are familiar with another case study research report, you can analyze this article instead. Notice that in two of the articles listed below, the researcher decided to organize the findings according to the individual participants. Using this type of organization allowed them to make comparisons and contrasts among their participants.

Articles

Fang, X., & Warschauer, M. (2004). Technology and curricular reform in China: A case study. *TESOL Quarterly, 38*(2), 301–324. (This study reports on a 5-year study of a technology-enhanced curricular reform project at one university in eastern China. Data include participant observation, interviews, surveys, and text analysis.)

Peirce, B. N. (1995). Social identity, investment and language learning. *TESOL Quarterly, 29*(1), 9–31. (This study examines how 5 immigrant women created, responded to, and resisted opportunities to speak English. Data include student diaries, questionnaires, individual and group interviews, and home visits.)

Kamhi-Stein, L. D. (2003). Reading in two languages: How attitudes toward home language and beliefs about reading affect the behaviors of "underprepared" L2 college readers. *TESOL Quarterly, 37*(1), 35–71. (This study examines 4 bilingual, native-Spanish-speaking female college freshman's L1 and L2 reading strategy as well as their attitudes toward their home language and beliefs about reading. Data include think-aloud protocols, open-ended interviews, self-assessment inventories, and reading comprehension measures.)

Questions

1. What is the research question?
2. In what context was the research conducted?
3. Who were the participants in the study? How were they selected? What were their relevant characteristics?
4. What was the theoretical orientation of the researcher?
5. What was the role of the researcher?
6. What data-collection procedures were used? How much time was spent collecting data?
7. How were data analyzed? What were the findings?
8. What conclusions are drawn? Are they logically related to the descriptive data?
9. What is the contribution of the study to our knowledge of social or contextual factors in second language learning?
10. What are the stated implications for teaching?

(Johnson, 1992, p. 91)

* * *

Ethnographic Studies

Defining Ethnographic Studies

Ethnography had its beginnings in anthropology. In the original sense, ethnographies were in-depth studies of particular cultures. More recently, however, more limited investigations of particular social contexts such as classrooms have been termed *interpretive qualitative studies* or *ethnographic studies*. We shall use the latter term in our discussion. In investigating a culture or a particular social context, ethnographers strive to obtain an emic perspective and a holistic view of what they are studying.

An *emic perspective* is an insider's view of a particular culture or community. In investigating the learning experience of a particular group of ESL students, a researcher would try to find out how these learners' view their own learning experiences. For example, in chapter 1, we reviewed the study by Willett in which she investigated the experiences of four L2 children enrolled in a mainstream first-grade classroom. Her overall aim was to understand how these children viewed their experiences in the mainstream classroom. In order to accomplish this task, Willett became a participant observer in the classroom, working as a teacher's aide. While in the classroom, she took field notes of events and critical incidents and audiotaped the children. During her 4-year ethnographic study she also took notes concerning the social and academic life of the school and community. Although she did not interview the children formally, she interacted with them daily and through casual conversations with them she was able to get an understanding of what was happening in the classroom from their perspective. She did all of these things in order to get an emic perspective of the students' experiences. This is in contrast to an *etic perspective* in which researchers interpret what they see largely from their own perspective.

Ethnographers also attempt to attain a *holistic view* of a particular social context by examining "what people say and what people do in a given context and across contexts in order to arrive at a fuller representation of what is going on" (Hornberger, 1994, p. 688). In order to achieve this holistic viewpoint, ethnographers doing L2 classroom research observe individual students in a variety of contexts and interview key individuals in these contexts to get multiple views of particular students. Willett, for example, studied the target children in a variety of situations in the school and worked with their families and teachers.

Achieving both a holistic and emic view of a particular context and its participants requires long-term observation; in fact, most ethnographies involve prolonged investigations of one or more years. This long period of engagement allows the researcher to conduct ongoing observations, to learn more about the community, and to check for any misinterpretations.

One of the key components of an ethnographic methodology is *triangulation*. Triangulation involves the use of multiple methods and/or multiple data sources in order to verify the researchers' interpretations of a community. For example, in studying a particular group of L2 learners, a researcher might observe the students in the classroom, with their peers outside the classroom, and at home with their families. They might also conduct in depth interviews with them as well as with their teachers, parents, and peers. All of this would be done in order to have multiple sources on which to build an interpretation of what is being studied.

One of the major limitations of ethnographic studies is how to strike a balance between the insider and outsider perspective. If teachers are too familiar with a teaching context, they have biases, which may distort their interpretations. On the other hand, if teachers are unfamiliar with a teaching context they may not be able to get an insider's view of the dynamics in the classroom. Striking a balance between these two extremes is challenging because as Hornberger (1994) points out, "classroom teachers researching their own culture must simultaneously maintain membership for the sake of their identity and detach themselves from the culture sufficiently to describe it" (pp. 689–690).

Doing Ethnographic Research

Observing Without Biases.   One of the key components of ethnographic research is observation. In order to gain an emic perspective a particular community, an ethnographer must carefully observe every aspect of a particular context for an extended period of time. In the process of observing, the ethnographer must, as Spradley (1980) suggests, set aside beliefs in

> *naïve realism*, the almost universal belief that all people define the *real* world of objects, events, and living creatures in pretty much the same way. . . . The naïve realist assumes that love, snow, marriage, worship, animals, death, food and hundreds of other things have essentially the same meaning to all human beings. Although few of us would admit to such ethnocentrism, the assumption may unconsciously influence our research. Ethnography starts with a conscious attitude of almost complete ignorance. (p. 4)

The ultimate goal of the ethnographer is to find out what actions and events mean to the people being observed.

What to Observe.   Richards (2003) maintains that there are four central components of observation in ethnographic research: the *setting, systems, people,* and *behavior.*

Within *the setting* a researcher needs to give attention to both space and objects. Richard suggests that in analyzing space, an observer sketch a particular setting and ask the following questions.

What space is available and how is it distributed? (*Distribution*) Are there distinct territories? Who inhabits them, who are the visitors and who is excluded? What are the rules relating to them? (*Territories*) Are particular activities related to particular spaces? Which spaces encourage particular activities and which spaces discourage them? How do people make use of the setting in their everyday activities? (*Activities*) Are there any spaces or rules relating to spaces that allow people to define themselves or their actions (e.g., Jo sitting at the resources desk means "I'm being the co-ordinator")? (*Roles*) (p, 131)

Applying these questions to a classroom, a researcher might ask:

1. What space is available in the classroom? Is certain space designated for particular functions? (Distribution)
2. Do certain individuals inhabit particular portions of the space? For example, is the teacher typically in one space and the students in other spots? (Territories)
3. Do certain activities take place in one place as opposed to another? Is there, for example, a particular place for less structured activities? (Activities)
4. Does certain space designate a specific role? Do students sitting in particular positions in the classroom have any specific roles? (Roles)

The second feature an ethnographer needs to observe is the *systems*, which can be both formal and informal. With formal systems the participants must follow a particular procedure. For example, in a classroom there might be a formal system for distributing books in which students get books in a pre-specified order or an informal system that allows students to select books on their own. There might also be a formal way of taking roll as opposed to a more informal way. Classrooms with more formal systems would be more structured.

The third element that needs to be observed is the *people* in the setting. Here Richards (2003) suggests that the observer consider what role each individual plays, what the relationship is between the actors in the setting, and what interactions and feelings are evident. In a classroom, a researcher would observe if particular students fulfill certain roles or if they interact with a particular group of students. This kind of observation would lead to identifying such things as peer groups and class leaders.

The fourth feature is *behavior*. In observing the behavior of the people in a classroom, Richards contends that it is important to observe several aspects of behavior including the timing, routines, and events. In terms of a classroom, *timing* is important since activities that occur at the beginning of a lesson may be of more significance than what happens later. The *routines* of the classroom establish a regular pattern of classroom behavior in which students expect certain activities to occur in a particular order in a classroom. Having another teacher would likely disturb this routine and challenge some of the usual roles students take. Finally, *events*, a set of related activities, provide the basis for routines. These could include vocabulary quizzes, listening tasks, or storytelling time.

How to Observe.   As is obvious from the preceding discussion, in undertaking observations of L2 teaching and learning, ethnographers need to focus on many aspects of the classroom. Given the immensity of the task, Richards (2003) suggests four possible strategies for observation. A researcher can start with one of these strategies and then shift to another strategy to get an alternative view of what is happening. The first strategy is to observe and record everything, which gives the observer a broad look at the environment. The second strategy is to observe and look for nothing in particular, which may lead the observer to notice unusual happenings. The third strategy is to look for paradoxes so that observers might notice that a student who is generally very quiet in the classroom, suddenly begins to be one of the most talkative members of the class. The final strategy is to identify the key problems facing a group. With this strategy the observer would focus on a particular classroom problem that seems to be occurring, such as a particular group of students generally not participating in classroom activities.

Taking Field Notes.   Taking thorough, descriptive field notes is essential for quality ethnographic studies because they provide a recording of what the researcher has seen and heard. Field notes should contain everything that the researcher believes is important. Whereas the style of note-taking can vary, with some researchers using shorthand or special notations, all researchers need to take careful notes, recording when and where the notes are taken, who was present, and what activities occurred. The notes also need to be stored in a safe location. Patton (1990) offers several suggestions for taking field notes.

1. Field notes should *be descriptive.* As he says, "no skill is more critical in field work than learning to be descriptive, concrete and detailed" (p. 241). Patton suggests that researchers avoid using general terms like "poor," "angry" or "uneasy" because these are interpretive rather than descriptive words. Instead the researcher should describe in as much detail as possible what individuals say, how they say it, and what gesture they use.

2. Field notes should *contain what people say.* If possible, researchers should write down exactly what individuals say so that this data can later be used to provide a rich description of what was observed.

3. Field notes should also *contain the researcher's own feelings and reactions* about what they observed. Whereas researchers need to give as objective an account of what they observe as possible, they should also include their reactions to what they see. Because in qualitative studies, researchers recognize that they cannot be completely objective, it is important that they recognize their own feelings about what they see.

4. Field notes should *include interpretations.* These interpretations and insights can aid researchers as they analyze all the data they have collected. Like the recording of their feelings, these notes should be kept separate from the descriptive account of what is observed.

Fieldworkers also need to be sensitive about when and where they take notes. If a researcher's goal is to establish a long-term relationship with a participant, it may be best to avoid note-taking in the initial part of the study. However, if researchers are observing as non-participant observers for a short time, then they might take notes right away.

Analyzing Data.   Because a great deal of data are gathered in ethnographic studies from field notes and interviews, data analysis can be time-consuming and tedious. As Patton (1990) notes, the challenge of data analysis "is to make sense of massive amounts of data, reduce the volume of information, identify significant patterns, and construct a framework for communicating the essence of what the data reveal" (pp. 371–372). There are various ways that researchers can approach the data analysis. Patton suggests several ways researchers might initially deal with data obtained from observations, among them the following.

1. *Chronology*—Researchers can organize their notes over time to basically tell a story of what they observed.
2. *Key events*—Researchers can organize the data by key events they observe and perhaps organize these events by their significance.
3. *Various settings*—Data can be organized according to where they occur.
4. *People*—If individuals or groups are the primary unit of analysis, then the data could be organized by cases.
5. *Issues*—Data can also be organized by key issues that the researcher has identified.

The choice of which approach to take depends on the judgment of the researcher. Ultimately, the quality of the research depends on these judgments. As Patton (1990) puts it, "because qualitative inquiry depends, at every stage, on the skills, training, insights, and capability of the researcher, qualitative analysis ultimately depends on the analytical intellect and style of the analyst" (p. 372).

In ethnographic studies the data analysis typically occurs over the course of the study, with researchers going back to the data as new insights and interpretations arise. The analysis is essentially an inductive cyclical process in which the ethnographer returns to the data over and over again to arrive at interpretations that are grounded in the data itself. In reporting the findings, the ethnographer strives to select representative rather than atypical examples to support specific conclusions. This is one important way to ensure the credibility of the research. Typically ethnographers provide what is termed *thick descriptions* or detailed accounts of what they observe, with many representative examples from the data. This is done so that readers can determine for themselves to what extent the conclusions reached in a particular study can be transferred to other similar contexts.

Ethnographic Classroom Research

As is evident from the previous discussion, ethnographic classroom research demands a great deal of time and commitment, involving a lot of record keeping, extensive participation in classrooms, and tedious analysis of multifaceted data. Because of this, the number of such studies is limited. However, those studies that exist present a rich and multidimensional view of students and teachers. Harklau (1994), for example, spent 3½ years examining the learning experience of 4 recently arrived Chinese immigrants as they made the transition from ESL to mainstream classrooms. Each of the focal students was observed through full school days in both ESL and mainstream classes and samples of their school work and homework were collected. In addition to informal discussions with the students, Harklau conducted between two and seven formal interviews of up to 1 hour with each of them. She also interviewed their teachers and observed other Chinese immigrants at the school to supplement her research. In total she conducted 315 hours of observation and 38 formal interviews.

Based on this data, Harklau characterized the differences between the ESL and mainstream classrooms in their use of spoken and written language, as well as classroom goals and structure. She also described the socializing features of the school as they existed in counseling and peer networks. She concludes that the main advantage of the mainstream classes was that there was a good deal of authentic input and communicative interaction. However, there was little opportunity for extended interaction and for explicit feedback on their use of English. In addition, although there were many social opportunities for using English with native speakers, the immigrants rarely took advantage of these situations and saw themselves as outsiders. On the other hand, the ESL classes provided the Chinese students with explicit language instruction and offered the students opportunities for counseling and peer interaction. However, the students viewed the ESL classes as easy and remedial, recognizing the stigma such classes had within the school as a whole. As Harklau points out, the value of such detailed ethnographic studies is that they provide educators with a basis for developing new programs for recently arrived immigrants that better meet their language, content, and social needs.

*   *   *

Exploring the Ideas, 2.12

Describe a general area of teaching and learning in an L2 classroom setting that you believe might be addressed in an ethnographic study. This might involve the role of L2 learners in mainstream classrooms or the peer group interactions of ESL students within a classroom setting. Select a classroom which you think might be productive setting to provide insight into this issue. Then observe two classes. Initially use the strategy described above in which you try to observe and record everything in the classroom to give you a broad look at the environment. Then shift to another one of the strategies described above. In your observations, keep in mind the four central components of observation mentioned above, namely, the *setting, systems, people,* and *behavior.*

Take careful field notes during your observations. As we discussed, try to make them descriptive, containing objective accounts of what people say and do. Also in a separate section of your notes include your feelings and interpretations of what you saw. If possible, compare your experience and notes with classmates or colleagues.

*   *   *

Exploring the Ideas, 2.13

Read one of the ethnographic studies listed below and then answer the questions that follow. If you are familiar with another ethnographic study, you can analyze this article instead.

Articles

Duff, P. (1995). An ethnography of communication in immersion classrooms in Hungary. *TESOL Quarterly, 29*(3), 505–536. (Duff provides a qualitative analysis of the changes in English language teaching and learning that occurred in Hungary within newly created English immersion schools.)

Flowerdew, J., & Miller, L. (1995). On the notion of culture in second language lectures. *TESOL Quarterly, 29*(2), 345–374. (Flowerdew and Miller investigate academic lectures at a university in Hong Kong to arrive at an understanding of the role of culture in these lectures.)

Toohey, K. (1998). "Breaking them up, taking them away": ESL students in grade 1. *TESOL Quarterly, 32*(1), 61–84. (Toohey describes a grade 1 classroom of L1 and L2 learners to delineate classroom practices that served to differentiate the participants and stratify the classroom.)

Questions

1. What was the overall goal of the ethnographic study?
2. Where was the study conducted?
3. Who were the participants of the study?
4. What was the role of the ethnographer? Was he/she a participant observer?
5. How long did the investigation take? What data were gathered?
6. How were the data analyzed?
7. What patterns were identified?
8. What conclusions were reached? Do they seem justified in light of the data that was presented?
9. What were the pedagogical implications of the study? Do they seem warranted in light of the findings of the study?

SUMMARY

In this chapter we examined how researchers can investigate teachers' and students' opinions, actions, and thoughts through the use of action research cycles, surveys, interviews, verbal reports, diary studies, case studies, and ethnographic studies. We began by pointing out that action research cycles offer a productive method for teachers to collaboratively investigate the problems they face in their own classrooms. To be considered action research, and not merely reflective teaching, teachers must gather and analyze data that can help solve classroom problems.

In discussing surveys, we examined the types of questions that can be used on surveys, noting the advantages and disadvantages of close-ended and open-ended questions. We pointed out several principles to keep in mind in writing survey questions so that they are clear and unbiased. We then explained various ways of displaying survey results gathered from close-ended questions, including raw numbers, percentages, means, and visual displays.

Our discussion of interviews included an explanation of the purposes of interviews and the type of interview formats that are possible. We emphasized the need to recognize the power relationship that exists in teacher–student interviews in both conducting an interview and in interpreting the data. We pointed out that one way to minimize the effect of this power relationship is to listen carefully and sympathetically to students during the interview. We also discussed ways to analyze interview data.

Next we examined how verbal reports and diary studies can be used to discover more about the thoughts of L2 teachers and learners. We pointed out the criticisms made about the methodology of verbal reports and suggested various principles to keep in mind when conducting a verbal report. Given the difficulty of developing a coding system for analyzing verbal report data, we suggested that researchers begin the data analysis process by reviewing existing coding systems. We then presented an example of a coding system for reading protocols. In investigating diary studies, we highlighted the importance of carefully analyzing the data contained in journal entries. We also discussed the benefits and drawbacks of conducting diary studies.

In the final section of the chapter we examined how case studies and ethnographic studies can be used to learn more about L2 teachers and learners. We noted the difficulty of defining case study research and outlined procedures for sound case study research. In discussing ethnographic studies, we emphasized how ethnographers try to gain an emic and holistic view of teachers and learners. We explained various strategies for observing L2 classrooms and highlighted the importance of taking thorough and descriptive field notes. We also pointed out some of the difficulties of data analysis and suggested several ways to organize ethnographic data.

FURTHER READING

On Action Research

Burns, A. (1999). *Collaborative action research for English teachers.* Cambridge, UK: Cambridge University Press.

Edge, J. (Ed.) (2001). *Action research.* Alexandria, VA: TESOL.

Freeman, D. (1998) *Doing teacher research.* New York: Heinle & Heinle Publishers.

Wallace, M. (1998). *Action research for language teachers.* Cambridge, UK: Cambridge University Press.

On Surveys

Brown, J. D. (2001). *Using surveys in language programs.* Cambridge, UK: Cambridge University Press.
Dornyei, Z. (2003). *Questionnaires in second language research.* Mahwah, NJ: Lawrence Erlbaum Associates.

On Interviews

Nunan, D. (1992). *Research methods in language learning.* Cambridge, UK: Cambridge University Press. (Chapter 7)
Patton, M. Q. (1990). *Qualitative evaluation and research methods.* Newbury Park, CA: Sage. (Chapter 7)
Richards, K. (2003). *Qualitative inquiry in TESOL.* New York: Palgrave MacMillan. (Chapter 2)

On Verbal Reports

Brown, J. D., & Rodgers, T. S. (2002). *Doing second language research.* Oxford, UK: Oxford University Press. (Chapter 3)
Ericsson, K. A., & Simon, H. A. (1993). *Protocol analysis.* Cambridge, MA: The MIT Press.
Gass, S., & Mackey, A. (2000). *Stimulated recall methodology in second language research.* Mahwah, NJ: Lawrence Erlbaum Associates.

On Diary Studies

Bailey, K. M., & Ochsner, R. (1983). A methodological review of the diary studies: Windmill tilting or social science? In K. M. Bailey, M. H. Long, & S. Peck (Eds.), *Second language acquisition studies* (pp. 188–198). Rowley, MA: Newbury House.
Bailey, K. M. (1990). The use of diary studies in teacher education programs. In J. C. Richards & D. Nunan (Eds.), *Second language teacher education* (pp. 215–240). Cambridge, UK: Cambridge University Press.
Bailey, K. M. (1991). Diary studies of classroom language learning: The doubting game and the believing game. In E. Sadtono (Ed.), *Language acquisition and the second/foreign language classroom* (pp. 60–102). Singapore: SEAMEO Regional Language Center.

On Case Studies

Johnson, D. (1992). *Approaches to research in second language learning.* New York: Longman. (Chapter 4)
Nunan, D. (1992). *Research methods in language learning.* Cambridge, UK: Cambridge University Press. (Chapter 4)
Yin, R. K. (2003). *Case study research design and method.* Thousand Oaks, CA: Sage.

On Ethnographic Studies

Fetterman, D. (1989). *Ethnography*. New York: Sage.

Johnson, D. (1992). *Approaches to research in second language learning*. New York: Longman. (Chapter 6)

Nunan, D. (1992). *Research methods in language learning*. Cambridge, UK: Cambridge University Press. (Chapter 3)

Patton, M. Q. (1990). *Qualitative evaluation and research methods*. Newbury Park, CA: Sage.

Richards, K. (2003). *Qualitative inquiry in TESOL*. New York: Palgrave MacMillan.

Spradley, J. P. (1980). *Participation observation*. New York: Holt, Rinehart & Winston.

Researching Classroom Discourse

In this chapter we explore the following questions:

- What are the assumptions and procedures of research methods commonly used to study the oral and written discourse of L2 classrooms?
- What are examples of such research?

In this chapter we begin by examining methods that can be used to study classroom oral discourse, namely, interaction analysis and discourse analysis. In the second part of the chapter we explore how text analysis can be used to study students' written texts, teachers' written feedback, and L2 classroom materials. We end the chapter by examining how corpus linguistics can be used to study written L2 classroom discourse.

ORAL DISCOURSE

Interaction Analysis

Defining Interaction Analysis

Interaction analysis uses some type of coding system to investigate the communication patterns that occur in a classroom. These coding systems can be used to

- determine what kind of classroom interaction best promotes L2 learning,

- evaluate teachers to determine whether or not they use patterns of communication that have been shown to be effective, and/or
- train prospective teachers to use a variety of communication patterns in their classrooms.

In the field of education there are over 200 different coding systems. They differ, however, in what classroom behaviors they try to account for. Some systems are very comprehensive with the purpose of describing all of the communication patterns that occur in a classroom. We term these *generic coding schemes*. Others are specialized so that they deal only with the moves that are used in a particular type of classroom interaction such as student–teacher conferences or group work. We term these *limited coding schemes*. In order to clarify what a coding system is and how the coverage of the system can differ we examine both types of coding systems.

Generic Coding Schemes

Generic coding schemes can vary along several dimensions, including the following (Chaudron, 1988).

1. *Recording Procedure:* In some coding systems, the observer codes a behavior every time it occurs, whereas in others they code only what is happening at a specified time period (e.g., every 30 seconds or every minute).
2. *Multiple Coding:* In some systems, the observer can assign more than one code to a particular behavior. For example, a behavior could be coded by pedagogical function (e.g., teacher praise) as well as modality (e.g., verbal or nonverbal). Although such coding patterns allow for multidimensional coding, because of their complexity, they can result in lower inter-rater reliability.

One of the most widely used generic coding systems is the Communicative Orientation of Language Teaching (COLT) designed by Allen, Fröhlich, and Spada (1984). The scheme was developed in the early 1980s as part of a large-scale Canadian research project to investigate the effects of particular instructional variables on the development of language proficiency. Because the goal of the project was to determine the effects of instruction on learning outcomes, some type of classroom observation scheme was needed to systematically describe what was happening in different L2 classrooms (Spada & Fröhlich, 1995). Because at that time there was widespread support of communicative language teacher (CLT), one aim of the project was to assess the influence of CLT on language development.

The scheme then needed to include categories that dealt with the communicative features of a classroom.

The scheme itself is divided into two parts: *Part A* describes *activities* of the classroom whereas *Part B* describes *the communicative features* of the exchange. In Part A the observer codes the following categories (Allen, Fröhlich, & Spada, 1984).

1. *Activity type* describes the kind of activity such as a drill, singing, discussion, and so on.
2. *Participation organization* indicates the participation pattern: whole class, group work, and group and individual work.
3. *Content* indicates whether the focus is on classroom management, on an explicit language focus, or on some other content. Also the category deals with whether or not the topic is controlled by the teacher, student, or is shared.
4. *Modality* identifies the skill type—listening, speaking, reading, writing, or a combination.
5. *Materials* indicates the type of material (i.e., text, audio, or visual), the length of the text, the purpose of the text (i.e., pedagogic, semi-pedagogic, or non-pedagogic), and the use of materials (i.e., highly controlled, semi-controlled, or minimally controlled).

Part B consists of an analysis of the communicative features occurring within each activity and includes the following subcategories.

1. *Use of the target language* measures the extent to which the target language is used.
2. *Information gap* refers to the extent to which the information that is dealt with is predictable and genuine.
3. *Sustained speech* deals with the extent to which the speaker engages in extended discourse.
4. *Reaction to code or message* refers to the extent to which the purpose of the exchange is on the accuracy of the message or the meaning.
5. *Incorporation of preceding utterances* refers to how a comment relates to the preceding comment, exemplifying no incorporation, repetition, paraphrase, comment, expansion, or elaboration.
6. *Discourse initiation* refers to whether the teacher or student initiates the exchange.
7. *Relative restriction of linguistic form* refers to the expected linguistic form of a response being either restricted use (one form is expected),

limited restriction, or unrestricted use (i.e., there is no expectation of any particular form).

The strength of the COLT scheme is that it includes categories that make it possible to examine the extent to which a class exhibits features of a communicative classroom. However, as with all coding schemes, by depending on prespecified categories, it may not capture the complexity of classroom discourse. Table 3.1 provides a grid that summarizes the overall components of the scheme. The table is based on a later work by Spada and Fröhlich (1995) and includes some minor changes from the earlier scheme.

*   *   *

Exploring the Ideas, 3.1

The following exercise illustrates how the COLT scheme works. The practice shown here demonstrates how an observer would code a particular interaction for predictable versus unpredictable information, one of the categories listed in Part B under Information Gap. The practice exercise is included in Spada and Fröhlich (1995), a practice manual designed to familiarize observers with the COLT Scheme.

Predictable information is information that is easily anticipated, whereas unpredictable information is not easily anticipated because there is a wider range of possibilities. These differences are evident in the coding of the following exchanges (Spada & Fröhlich, 1995, p. 69) .

Example 1

Teacher and student speech	Coding
T: What's the past tense of 'I go'?	Pseudo request
S: I goed	Giving predictable information (although information is incorrect)

Example 2

Teacher and student speech	Coding
T: Does anyone know when Jose's birthday is?	Genuine request
S: I think it's the 24th.	Giving unpredictable information (although information is incorrect)

S2: No, it's the 25th; I know because it was my birthday on the 26th and I know hers is the day before mine.

TABLE 3.1
The COLT System

Communicative Orientation of Language Teaching (COLT): Part A

SCHOOL
TEACHER
SUBJECT

GRADE(S)
LESSON (Minutes)

DATE
OBSERVER

| Col. 1 | 2 | 3 | 4 | 5 | 6 | 7 | 8 | 9 | 10 | 11 | 12 | 13 | 14 | 15 | 16 | 17 | 18 | 19 | 20 | 21 | 22 | 23 | 24 | 25 | 26 | 27 | 28 | 29 | 30 | 31 | 32 | 33 | 34 | 35 | 36 | 37 | 38 | 39 | 40 | 41 | 42 | 43 | 44 | 45 | 46 | 47 | 48 |

PARTIC. ORGANIZATION

CONTENT

STUDENT MODALITY

MATERIALS

TIME — ACTIVITIES

Participant Organization:
- Class: T s/c, S s/c, Choral
- Group: Same, Different
- Comb.: Individual, Gr/Ind.
- MAN.: Procedure, Discipline

Content:
- LANGUAGE: Form, Function, Discourse, Socioling.
- OTHER TOPICS:
  - NARROW: Classroom, Stereotyp., Pers/Bio., Other
  - LIMITED: Personal, Rout./Soc., Fam./Com., School T., Other
  - BROAD: Abstract, Pers./Ref., Imagination, World T., Other
- TOPIC CONTROL: Teacher, Teacher/Stud., Student

Student Modality: Listening, Speaking, Reading, Writing, Other

Materials:
- Type:
  - Text: Minimal, Extended
  - Audio
  - Visual
  - Pedagogic
  - Semi-Pedag.
  - Non-Pedag.
- Use: High Control, Semi Control, Mini Control

(Continued)

93

TABLE 3.1
(Continued)

Communicative Orientation of Language Teaching (COLT): Part B

				STUDENT VERBAL INTERACTION						
INCORPORATION of S/T UTTERANCES	Elaboration									
	Expansion									
	Comment									
	Paraphrase									
	Repetition									
	No Incorp.									
REACTION CO/MES.	Explicit Code Reaction									
FORM RESTR.	Unrestricted									
	Limited									
	Restricted									
SUST. SPEECH	Sustained									
	Minimal									
	Ultraminimal									
INFORMATION GAP	Request Info. — Genuine									
	Request Info. — Pseudo									
	Giving Info. — Unpred.									
	Giving Info. — Pred.									
TARGET LANG.	Disc.-Initiation									
	L₂									
	L₁									
	Choral									

					TEACHER VERBAL INTERACTION					
INCORPORATION of S. UTTERANCES	Elaboration									
	Expansion									
	Comment									
	Paraphrase									
	Repetition									
	No Incorp.									
REACTION CO/MES.	Explicit Code Reaction									
SUST. SPEECH	Sustained									
	Minimal									
INFORMATION GAP	Request Info. — Genuine									
	Request Info. — Pseudo									
	Giving Info. — Unpred.									
	Giving Info. — Predict.									
TARGET LANG.	L₂									
	L₁									
COMMUNIC. FEATURES	Off-task									
	No talk									

(Spada & Fröhlich, 1995, front and back cover)

Look at the excerpts of classroom speech below and decide whether each turn should be coded as *Predictable* or *Unpredictable* information. Code only the student turns that are underlined.

1. Situation: The students are being assigned class jobs for the day. To assign the jobs, the teacher is drawing students' names from a hat and asking them each a question. The students have to answer one question correctly to get a class job.

Teacher and student speech	**Coding**

T: Uh, David, give me the name of two stores in
    Asbestos (the name of the town in which
    the students live).

S: Uh, Continental.

T: Continental is one store.

S: Canadian Tire.

T: Boy, David is wide awake this morning.

2. Situation: The teacher is talking with the students about having papers signed by their parents.

Teacher and student speech	**Coding**

T: I want your paper here at one o'clock
    this afternoon absolutely.

S: I can't by then.

T: Why?

S: My, my father's working.

T: Did you check with your parents yesterday?

S: He's a teacher.

(Source: Spada & Fröhlich, 1995, p. 70)

* * *

Brown and Rodgers (2002) offer a variety of criticisms of generic coding schemes, including the following:

- The huge range of schemes available (over 200) means that exposure to one or two of these does not provide a good deal of insight into the range of schemes available.
- Most of the instruments require considerable training to use.
- Transcription and analysis of observational data is a tedious process.

- Whereas classroom observation schemes were popular in the 1960s and 1970s, their practice declined due to a variety of criticisms regarding their cumbersome design.
- The fact that there are so many instruments available makes it difficult to compare the results of existing studies.
- It is challenging to find classes that can be observed over a long period of time.
- Classroom observation schemes reflect the biases of a particular researcher. Given the lack of consensus as to what constitutes effective teaching, it is difficult to recommend any one scheme.

In view of these shortcomings of generic coding schemes, one alternative is to design more limited coding schemes that are tailored to a specific classroom discourse type such as writing conferences or peer review. A second possibility is to design a coding scheme that deals with just one aspect of classroom interaction, such as teachers' error correction strategies or the type of questions teachers use.

Limited Coding Systems

With a limited coding systems, the categories are developed in reference to a specific classroom activity. Brown and Rodgers (2002), for example, provide a coding system that could be used with a picture-sequencing task. In this type of task, students are provided with a set of pictures that tell a story. With a partner, students are to decide on a logical sequence for the pictures. Table 3.2 illustrates categories that could be used to analyze the moves that would typically occur in such an activity.

TABLE 3.2
Interaction Codes for Cooperative Picture Ordering Task

	Code	Example
Describes a Picture	D	There's a clock on the wall that says 8:00.
Proposal w/o Reasoning	P-	I think picture C should go first.
Proposal w/ Reasoning	P+	I think picture C should go first because the sun is coming up.
Support	S	Looks right. I agree. What's next?
Non-support	N	Nope, Unh, unh, Don't think so. Some other.
Counter-Proposal w/o Reasoning	CP-	No, I think B is first.
Counter-proposal w/Reasoning	CP+	But everybody's happy in B. I think it should go first.
Filler, Doubt, Neutral	F	Mmmm. Maybe. Let's see.
Operational	0	What do we have to do? Shall I start? Are we done?

(Source: Brown and Rodgers, 2002, p. 86).

Interaction Analysis Research

One example of an interaction analysis study using a limited coding system is Goldstein and Conrad's (1990) study of writing conferences. The study was designed to answer the following questions:

1. To what extent do ESL writing conferences ensure student input?
2. To what extent is meaning negotiated in ESL writing conferences?
3. What is the relationship between the discourse in the conference and successful revision in the subsequent draft? (p. 446)

The study involved 3 students from different cultural backgrounds of roughly equivalent proficiency who were in their last course of an ESL sequence that led to Freshman Composition. The data consisted of 10 20-minute conferences and two drafts of each of 10 papers. Based on several analyses of the data, Goldstein and Conrad identified seven features that they believed adequately characterized the conference data. These are listed in Table 3.3. They then calculated the frequency per conference of each of the categories listed below and computed the mean frequencies per category for each student's conference.

Goldstein and Conrad (1990) used this scheme to compare how the role of individual students in a writing conference differed. They found that students differed greatly in the amount of input they contributed to the conference and the degree to which they set the conference agenda. Although some students contributed almost half of the topic nominations, others contributed only one fifth. Students also differed in the degree to which they negotiated revisions in their essays. These differences in the degree of negotiation of revisions was important because Goldstein and Conrad found that when students negotiated revisions, they were more likely to successfully revise their essays.

Goldstein and Conrad (1990) conclude that "while a student *may* contribute input to the conference, *may* set the agenda, and *may* negotiate meaning, these are not guaranteed—even with the same teacher" (p. 455). It is possible that the teachers' role produced the variation in conferences so that teachers adjusted their style to the students' discourse style or to their expectations of the student. Whatever the cause of such differences, it was clear that having a conference that involved a negotiation of meaning led to more successful student revisions.

What is important to note from a methodological perspective is that Goldstein and Conrad's coding system was specifically designed to capture the patterns that occurred in writing conferences. Having such a fine-tuned coding system allowed them to draw conclusions regarding the roles of teachers and students in writing conferences and the importance of the ne-

TABLE 3.3
Discourse Features of Writing Conferences

1. *Episodes* These are the subunits of a conference. Each episode has a unique combination of topic and purpose.
2. *Discourse Structure* Each episode has a particular discourse structure.
   1. Teacher talks and student backchannels.
   2. Teacher questions and student answers.
   3. Teacher talks and student talks.
   4. Student talks and teacher backchannels.
   5. Student questions and teacher answers.
   6. A combination of the above.
3. *Topic Nomination* The participant who introduces a new topic or new purpose is said to have nominated the topic of a new episode.
4. *Invited Nomination* An invited nomination occurs when the participant nominates the topic in response to a question, such as "What would you like to discuss?"
5. *Turns* A change of speaker signifies a new turn.
6. *Questions* This category includes all questions except those used for negotiation.
7. *Negotiation* Two types of negotiation exist.
   • *Negotiation of meaning* includes confirmation checks, comprehension checks, and clarification requests.
   • *Negotiation of revision* takes place when revision strategies need to be clarified and consists of
   a. the student confirming the teacher's suggestion for revision;
   b. either the teacher or student checking to see if the student understands discussion of revision options;
   c. the student checking to see if it would be appropriate to revise in a certain way; or
   d. the student stating that he/she does not understand either why a revision is necessary or how to revise.

(Adapted from Goldstein and Conrad, 1990, p. 448.)

gotiation of meaning in students' essay revisions. By selecting one aspect of classroom interaction you wish to investigate, you can design a coding system that is more finely tuned than the generic codes we looked at earlier. Your coding system should be based on an analyses of the interaction you observed, with the coding categories developing from the data. This inductive process is in sharp contrast to the deductive application of pre-existing categories employed in most generic coding systems.

* * *

Exploring the Ideas, 3.2

Listed next is an excerpt from a student teacher writing conference from an advanced level ESL university composition class. The data are part of a study conducted by Igarashi (2003) on writing conferences in college ESL classes. As a way of gaining practice in coding data according to an interaction coding scheme, analyze the discourse using the discourse features outlined above in the Goldstein and Conrad (1990) study. This episode deals with the student's phrasing of his essay thesis. Notice how some segments can be categorized into more than one category. A possible analysis of the first lines is shown here.

1 T: What would you like to talk about your paper today? (*Topic nomination, also teacher question and student answer*)

2 S: Um, this thesis, um, there are three reasons why a doctor should do what he thinks the best care for the patient, but what his patient thinks the best care for themselves. What I wanna know about that thesis is, I like kind of brief and short thesis. (*Invited nomination*)

1 T: What would you like to talk about your paper today?

2 S: Um, this thesis, um, there are three reasons why a doctor should do what he thinks the best care for the patient, but what his patient thinks the best care for themselves. What I wanna know about that thesis is, I like kind of brief and short thesis.

3 T: Uh huh, I know.

4 S: As you told in our class, in this 310 class, we don't have to put our thesis in one sentence.

5 T: Yes. You could say a thesis is not a list.

6 S: Yeah. And um, I wonder um, if I can use like this there are three reasons and first, second, third.

7 T: So what are the reasons?

8 S: Uh, first.

9 T: You can just tell me.

10 S: Uh, patients are not experts in medical care.

11 T: Uh huh.

12 S: Second, uh, teaching, uh, doctoring is a professional job such as teaching. That, that means doctor, uh, a doctor has to try, uh, for the best result.

13 T: Uh huh.

14 S: But uh, this patient, like, I mean, but he doesn't have to amuse his patient, just like teachers.

15 T: Amuse?

16 S: Yes, amuse.

17 T: Amuse. Okay.

18 S: Just like a teacher, like, uh, I showed an example that like, even though the students do not like to take exams.

19 T: Uh huh.

20 S: Still the teacher gives, uh, his students exams and grades because uh as a result, uh the methods have the students to improve their education.

21 T: Uh huh.

22 S: So it's like, just like, doctors has to do uh, things for his patient's health care, even though the, um, patient might not like it.

23 T: Right.

24 S: Yeah. The third is doctors also have rules and directions to follow.

25 T: What kind of rules?

26 S: The rules that he learned in medical school.

27 T: Uh.

28 S: So, like, general doctors school.

29 T: Uh huh.

30 S: So, now ((unintelligible))

31 T: So, your question is about the thesis now, right?

32 S: Yeah.

33 T: Okay. Basically you're saying, tell me, tell me if I'm wrong right here, that like you're answering the question, You know, what should, what should doctors do when the standard of medical, medical care comes to conflict with the patients. You say doctors should do with what they think is best. But it's more you have here. You think it's, they should do it because they are experts in their medical care. They are professionals, and they have rules they have to follow.

34 S: Yes.

35 T: Right? My opinion, my opinion is that if you said a little more what you really mean.

36 S: Uh huh.

37 T: Like what you just said.

38 S: Uh huh.

39 T: That your thesis will be more clear. Like you say here, ((reads)) *there are three reasons why doctors should do what he thinks is the best care for patients.* I'll just stop right there.

40 S: Uh huh.

41 T: Okay. All kinds of questions come out into my mind when I'm a reader, of course, I say, what are the three reasons? Right? Then I'm gonna ask for why. Why should the doctor do this? You're telling me that it's because the doctor is the professional, the doctor knows best.

42 S: Uh huh.

43 T: Right? I think you should say that.

44 S: I see.

*   *   *

Discourse Analysis

Defining Discourse Analysis

Discourse analysis has been variously defined but typically attention is given to the discourse context of interactions. McCarthy (1991), for example, maintains that "discourse analysis is concerned with the study of the relationship between language and the contexts in which it is used" (p. 5). Celce-Murcia and Olshtain (2000) define it as "the study of language in use that extends beyond sentence boundaries" (p. 4).

Discourse analysis developed in the 1960s and 1970s from work in various fields and tended to include two parallel interests: "text linguistics, which focused on written texts from a variety of fields and genres, and discourse analysis, which entailed a more cognitive and social perspective on language use and communication exchanges and which included spoken as well as written discourse" (Celce-Murcia & Olshtain, 2000, p. 4). For our purposes, we will focus on the latter area with an emphasis on spoken discourse.

Conversation Analysis.   As Lazaraton (2002) points out, the majority of L2 discourse analysis studies typically employ one of two qualitative research methodologies: *conversation analysis* (CA) or *ethnography of communication.* Conversation analysis involves an examination of naturally occurring talk in order to determine what is being accomplished for the speakers involved. For those doing CA and "trying to understand a bit of talk, the key question about any of its aspects is—*why that now?* . . . What is getting done by virtue of that bit of conduct, done that way, in just that place?" (Schegloff, Koshik, Jacoby, & Olsher, 2002, p. 5).

CA does not deal exclusively with conversations in the sense of interactions for sociability. Rather it can deal with a variety of interactions such as medical consultations or classroom interaction. Take, for example, the following medical interaction.

Pt: This- chemotherapy (0.2) it won't have any lasting effects on havin'
     kids will it?
     (2.2)

Pt: It will?

Dr: I'm afraid so.

(Source: Have, 1999, p. 4)

The goal of the conversation analyst is to investigate what is being accomplished for the speakers of this interaction. Have (1999) analyzes the interaction as follows:

> The patient proposes an optimistic assessment as to the effect of her forthcoming chemotherapy, after which the physician is silent, leading to a remarkably long, 2.2-second pause. In so doing, he can be seen as demonstrating that he is not able to endorse this positive assessment. Thereupon, the patient 'reverses' her statement in a questioning manner, 'It will?', which the doctor then does confirm with: 'I'm afraid so'. (p. 5)

In terms of methodology, conversation analysts generally adhere to the following principles (Lazaraton, 2002, pp. 37–38):

1. using authentic, recorded data which are carefully transcribed;
2. using "unmotivated looking" rather than prestated research questions;
3. employing the "turn" as the unit of analysis;
4. analyzing single cases, deviant cases, and collections thereof;
5. disregarding ethnographic and demographic particulars of the context and participants;
6. eschewing the coding and quantification of data.

Let us examine how these principles would be applied to an analysis of the interaction previously listed. First, the interaction is authentic, recorded data. Although the pauses are included, a fully transcribed interaction would include additional features of speech production. Second, the analysis involves "unmotivated looking." In other words, the researcher is not examining the discourse to answer a predetermined research question. Finally, the conversation analyst is not concerned with the social context of the interaction and, unlike interaction analysis, does not code and quantify the data.

Ethnography of Communication. The second major qualitative approach to discourse analysis is termed the *ethnography of communication*, which, as with all ethnographic research, recognizes the influence of culture and social realities in seeking to find holistic explanations for meaning and behavior. For Lazaraton (2002) the most salient difference between conversation analysis and the ethnography of communication is that the latter considers transcribed interactional data as "just one (and not necessarily the most important) source of information that should be considered in documenting cultural practices" (p. 40). In other words, the ethnographer of communication is concerned with the social context of the interaction and with achieving an emic and holistic perspective of the interaction. In an attempt to achieve a holistic explanation of a classroom exchange, ethnographers of communication might use interviews, classroom observations, field notes, and other data in their study. In general most of the qualitative discourse analysis studies of interest to L2 researchers and practitioners adhere to the principles of the ethnography of communication. This is because, as Schegloff, Koshik, Jacoby, and Olsher (2002) point out, "most CA research, including some research on talk in educational institutions, is not built to answer theoretically motivated research questions of the type that applied linguists often ask" (p. 14). In our discussion of discourse analysis we provide examples of ethnographies of communication.

Doing Discourse Analysis

Transcriptions.   For both conversation analysis and the ethnography of communication, natural interaction needs to be recorded and transcribed. Whereas it may seem that transcribing is a very simple process of writing down what is said, Have (1999) argues that a transcription is best seen as a "*translation,* made for various practical purposes, of the actually produced *speech* into a version of the standardized *language* of that particular community, with some selective indication of the actual speech production" (p. 76). Because spoken language conveys a good deal of meaning through intonation, pauses, overlaps, and so on, which cannot be fully captured in the written word, transcripts cannot be taken as equal to the recordings of spoken language. For this reason, Have (1999) contends that transcripts should not be considered as the data of discourse analysis; rather the recording itself is what the researcher must consider. What the researcher does in the process of transcribing the recording is to present a selective portion of the recording.

In an attempt to capture some of the features of spoken interaction, transcriptionists rely on coding systems that symbolize several features of spoken interaction. The following are some commonly used transcription symbols (adapted from Atkinson & Heritage, 1984; Have, 1999):

Sequencing

[A left bracket indicates the beginning of an overlap in speech.

]   A right bracket indicates the end of an overlap in speech.

=   An equal sign at the end of one line and an equal sign at the beginning of another indicates that there is no gap between the lines. This is called *latching.*

Timed Intervals

(.)   A period in parentheses indicates a micropause, that is, a pause of less than .2 second.

(0.0)   Numbers in parentheses indicate the length of a pause by tenths of a second.

Characteristics of Speech Production

Word   Underlining indicates some form of stress from pitch or loudness.

:   A colon indicates a lengthened sound or syllable. More colons indicate a more prolonged sound.

-       A dash indicates a cutoff, usually a glottal stop.

.   A period indicates falling intonation.

,   A comma indicates continuing intonation.

?   A question mark indicates a rising intonation.

.hhh   This symbol indicates inhalation.

hhh   This symbol indicates exhalation.

Transcriber's Doubts and Comments

( )   Empty parentheses indicates the transcriber's inability to hear what was said.

(( ))   Double parentheses indicates the transcriber's description of details of the scene.

Analyzing Transcripts.   Once recordings are transcribed, the researcher begins the task of analyzing the data by searching for patterns and explaining the logic of the interaction. In order to accomplish this, the researcher starts with a process of "unmotivated looking," which entails noticing what may at first seem unremarkable features of the interaction. The idea is to approach the data with an open mind and not with any preconceived ideas of what the data mean. Starting with an open mind, Have (1999) suggests that researchers undertake the following steps.

- First, a sequence of the interaction needs to be selected for analysis as was done with the previously mentioned medical consultation.
- Next the researcher needs to characterize the actions in the sequence on a turn-by-turn basis by considering what the participants are doing in each turn. In order to accomplish this task, the researcher considers "how the timing and taking of turns provide for certain understandings of the actions and matters being talked about" (Have, 1999, p. 106).
- Finally, the researcher considers how the manner in which the actions were accomplished reflects certain identities, roles, and relationships for the participants.

The advantage of using discourse analysis to investigate classroom interaction is that it allows researchers to gain insight into what is being accomplished in a particular classroom interaction that takes place in a specific social context. As Kumaravadivelu (1999) notes, by emphasizing the social context of language use, classroom discourse analysts can "look at the classroom event as a social event and the classroom as a minisociety with its own rules and regulations, routines and rituals. Their focus is the experience of teachers and learners within this minisociety" (p. 458).

Discourse Analysis Research

One example of a classroom discourse analysis study in an EFL setting is Hancock (1997). In this study, Hancock investigated how learners in a private language school in Madrid performed two role plays: one set in a restaurant in which one learner was a waiter and the other a customer and another in a guesthouse in which one learner was the landlady and the other the guest.

Hancock found that in the role plays students shifted between a *literal frame* in which they were behaving as themselves and a *nonliteral frame* in which they were role playing. The language used in the literal frame was off-record between the learners themselves and was often in Spanish. The language in the nonliteral frame, on the other hand, was on-record to be heard by a potential audience and was typically in English, the target language. The off-record exchanges typically dealt with questions about the task itself or the language. The following exchange illustrates how in an off-record or literal frame, Spanish was used to clarify the task (off-record is in bold):

1 G   do you like to have a shower?
2 MM yes please . . .
3   *eso lo preguntava yo* [**I was going to ask that**]
4 **G**   *no*
5 **MM** *es para mi* [**it's for me**]
6   can I have a shower (p. 225)

The second example illustrates how Spanish was occasionally used in the off-record frame to ask how something is said in English (off-record is in bold).

1 **Ev**   *que digo* [**what shall I say**]
2 **Er**   {**anything else?**
3 Ev   anything else? (p. 222)

Based on his analysis of the language used in these role plays, Hancock argues that teachers should not assume that all use of the L1 is bad and that use of the L2 is good. Rather sometimes the use of the mother tongue is a natural by-product of the interaction. Furthermore, attempts to stop such use of the L1 may be very difficult. The value of such studies is that, unlike coding systems that record only whether or not the L1 is used in the classroom or not, classroom discourse analysis can demonstrate the purposes L1 serves for the participants themselves. The study exemplifies how the meaning of an interaction is shaped by what precedes it and follows it and that every detail is purposeful and relevant.

A second example of a discourse analysis study focused on L2 learning is the investigation is Nakahama, Tyler, and van Lier (2001). In this study the researchers investigated how meaning is negotiated between native speakers (NSs) and nonnative speakers (NNSs) in two-way information-gap tasks as opposed to relatively unstructured conversations. The participants for the study were 3 Japanese females enrolled in an intermediate-level ESL university class and 3 female graduate students in linguistics. Each NS and NNS dyad interacted in a spot-the-difference information gap activity and a relatively unstructured conversation in which they discussed their common experiences at the university, their experiences living in the same city, and their common interests.

Part of the data analysis involved examining the discourse strategies used in each type of activity. For example, the researchers examined discourse strategies such as silence, the use of *okay*, the use of *oh*, and negotiation cycles. Previous research has shown that *oh* is frequently used to signal mutual understanding. In this study, the researchers found that in conversational activities, *oh* was quite frequently used for this purpose (112 times by NSs and 38 times by NNSs). The following excerpt from the conversational data illustrates how *oh* can be used to indicate understanding.

In a prior conversation, Mika (a NNS) mistakenly thought Donna (a NS) had asked her how long she would stay in the United States so she answered "for a year," whereas in reality Donna had asked her how long she had been in the United States. However, later in the conversation, Mika's answer did not make sense to Donna so she asked for clarification. In this excerpt Donna uses *oh* to show her understanding that Mika has not been in the United States for a year but only recently arrived.

60 Donna: But you were here last spring for the um..
61 Mika: Naa.
62 Donna: You were already here
63 Mika: I came here umm this umm this um January 2
64' Donna: <u>Oh</u> just January <u>Oh</u> so you haven't been here for one year you've been you're going to

65 Mika: From
66 Donna: stay for a year
67 Mika: A ya (p. 397)

Such data analysis, as opposed to purely quantitative analysis, allows researchers to examine how particular features are used in a specific context
and thus to reach conclusions about language use. The analysis is based on
the assumption that "there is no a priori justification for believing that any
detail of conversation, however minute, is disorderly, accidental or irrele-
vant" (Markee, 2000, p. 40). In this case, the particle *oh* was a key mecha-
nism for showing Donna's understanding of the situation.

Critical Discourse Analysis

One criticism of discourse analysis is that while it does examine the
sociolinguistic and sociocultural aspect of language use, it devotes no attention to the sociopolitical dimension of language use. Kumaravadivelu
(1999), for one, argues that classroom discourse analysis is limited because
it neglects to examine how the larger social and political framework influences what is said in the classroom. In order to overcome this shortcoming
he advocates a critical approach to classroom discourse analysis. He maintains that critical classroom discourse analysis (CCDA) is based on various
premises and principles including the premise that social, political, and historical conditions influence the interaction between teachers and learners
and that the L2 classroom "is not a secluded, self-contained minisociety; it is
rather a constituent of the larger society in which many forms of domina-
tion and inequality are produced and reproduced for the benefit of vested
interests" (p. 472).

One example of how critical discourse analysis can be applied to classroom interaction is Chick (1996), who examined the interactions of a native South African English-speaking (SAE) professor with his ethnically diverse students in a post-apartheid South Africa. Based on his data, Chick
maintains that in some instances Zulu students, unlike some of the SAE students, did not share the professor's understanding of the purpose of various educational routines. For example, in South African universities, post-
examination interviews are common. Many SAE professors, as well as SAE
students, see the interviews as a chance for teachers and students to discuss
students' preparation and performance on a university examination. On
the other hand, some Zulu students see the interview as a time to account
for their performance on the exam. Hence, the SAE professor and Zulu students have cross purposes in the interviews. Chick's analysis of the discourse of the interviews illustrates how the SAE and Zulu students' different
views of the purpose of the interview affected the interaction. The SAE stu-

dents tended to support the professor's idea that the interview was one of solidarity in which teacher and student were meeting to discuss their performance on the examination. This perspective is evident in the following exchange.

Student: Now I don't think I did this essay um answered that question entirely in that frame of reference.

Professor: Ya.

Student: I think that is what you're going to say.

Professor: Well, well, I'm I'm wanting to see.

Student: You're you're going to say I didn't actually um answer the essay in relation . . . (p. 341)

A Zulu student, on the other hand, who believed the interview as a place to justify his performance, took a role of deference and politeness as is evident in the following example in which the Zulu student uses the address term *sir*.

Professor: You mean . . . you didn't have the reading. . . .
             [Or you didn't know what the reading was . . .

Student: [(*starts to speak*) Yes sir

[= overlapping speech   (p. 340)

Chick contends that by using this politeness, the student unknowingly challenged the professor's assumption that the meeting was one of equitable relations and thus, he was probably more negatively evaluated by the professor. Chick goes on to argue that in post-apartheid South Africa such intercultural miscommunications can have serious consequences in terms of access to jobs, social welfare, and educational opportunities, where success often depends on sharing the communicative assumptions of power holders. The value of critical discourse analysis research is that it explicitly acknowledges and analyzes the power relationships that exist in a classroom.

* * *

Exploring the Ideas, 3.3

Read one of the discourse analysis studies listed here and then answer the questions that follow. If you are familiar with another discourse analysis study, you can analyze this article instead.

Articles:

Lazaraton, A. (2003). Incidental displays of cultural knowledge in the nonnative-English-speaking teacher's classroom. *TESOL Quarterly, 37*(2), 213–246. (This study examines the cultural knowledge shown by two nonnative-English-speaking teachers in their intensive English classroom.)

Nakahama, Y., Tyler, A., & van Lier, L. (2001). Negotiation of meaning in conversational and information gap activities: A comparative discourse analysis. *TESOL Quarterly, 35*(3), 377–405. (This study contrasts how meaning is negotiated in two different types of interactions between native English speakers and nonnative English speakers in a relatively unstructured conversation and a two-way information gap activity.)

Ulichny, P. (1996). Performed conversations in an ESL classroom. *TESOL Quarterly, 30*(4), 739–764. (This study employs discourse analysis to demonstrate how classroom interaction can combine the goals of negotiation of meaning and explicit instruction on the formal features of language.)

Questions:

1. What theoretical orientation informed the study?
2. Where was the study conducted?
3. Who were the participants of the study?
4. How were the data collected?
5. How were the data analyzed?
6. Is there any additional information you would like to have about the methodology used in the study?
7. What were the findings of the study? Do they seem justified in light of the data that were presented?
8. What were the pedagogical implications of the studies? Do they seem warranted in view of the findings of the study?

Be prepared to share your assessment of the article with your classmates.

* * *

WRITTEN DISCOURSE

Text Analysis of Student Texts

Defining Text Analysis

The field of text analysis developed during the 1970s and 1980s from a growing recognition that the traditional analysis of written texts from a largely morphological and syntactic perspective did not do justice to the complexity of written texts. Instead, as Grabe and Kaplan (1996) note, text researchers began to recognize that a "text is a multidimensional construct; that is, no unidimensional analysis of text can offer an adequate interpretation of the nature of text" (p. 39). The growing recognition of the complex nature of effective writing resulted in the development of text analysis, which Connor (1994) defines in the following way.

> Text analysis describes texts and evaluates their quality, both from the viewpoint of texts that learners produce as well as the kind of texts they need to produce. Text analysis can help ESL researchers, teachers, and language learners identify rules and principles of written or spoken texts at a variety of levels: sentences, sentence relations, and complete texts. This research orientation differs from traditional linguistic analysis in two major ways: (a) It extends analysis beyond the level of sentence grammar, and (b) it considers the multidimensional, communicative constraints of the situation. (p. 682)

Although those who support text analysis recognize the multidimensional nature of texts, some text analysts do isolate aspects of student texts such as verb choice and syntactic structure in an effort to contrast the writing style of proficient and non-proficient writers for the purpose of identifying typical features of effective texts.

Doing Syntactic Analysis of L2 Student Texts

Hyland (2002), among others, has argued for the importance of undertaking text analysis studies because such studies "can help us to understand both the features of effective writing and the influences that contribute to it" (p. 152). He lists various researchable questions on student texts, three of which are particularly relevant to our discussion:

- What features characterize the texts of this specific group of learners?
- Do these features differ from those in texts produced by other writers?
- Can these differences be explained by reference to language proficiency or L1 conventions? (p. 153)

Many studies that focus on the syntactic and lexical features of student texts address the questions listed above. Their purpose is to compare the linguistic features of texts written by L2 writers with those of L1 writers. The problem, of course, is to determine which features to analyze.

One of the early means used to examine the syntactic features of L1 student essays was what Hunt (1965) termed *T-units*. A T-unit is composed of a main clause and all of the dependent modifying clauses. For example, the sentence, "The student, who has taken several writing courses, still has problems with writing," would be considered as one T-unit. On the other hand, the sentence, "The student has taken several writing courses, but he still has problems with writing," is composed of two T-units. Hunt proposed that in determining T-units the researcher should ignore the student's punctuation and instead cut up the text into "the shortest segments which it would be grammatically allowable to write with a capital letter at one end and a period or a question mark at the other, leaving no fragment as residue" (p. 27). Several measures of syntactic maturity have been developed using the T-unit including the (a) number of words per T-unit; (b) the number of T-units per sentence; (c) the number of clauses per T-unit; and (d) the number of words per clause. Employing these measures as a way of assessing the syntactic maturity of L1 writers, Hunt (1965) showed that students in grades 4, 8, and 12 showed an increase in their syntactic development as expressed in T-units.

When T-unit analysis was applied to L2 student essays, some researchers argued that T-units were not suitable for use with low proficiency students. Homburg (1984), for one, argued that with low proficiency students it is necessary to recognize students' punctuation in segmenting the text. Thus, he defined a sentence "as a string of words with a capital letter at the beginning of the first word and a period or another terminal punctuation mark after the last word" (pp. 91–92). T-unit analysis of L2 essays also began to include the concept of error free T-units, which seemed to discriminate more accurately among various levels of syntactic maturity, namely, grammatical accuracy and complexity.

Syntactic Text Analysis Research

Ishikawa (1995) is one study that employs error-free T-unit analysis with low proficiency EFL students. The subjects were two classes of freshmen at a Japanese women's college. Students in both classes were given a homework task based on picture stories. For the first task, students were given a series of questions to elicit the story, resulting in a guided writing task. In the second task, the students wrote out the full story based on the pictures alone with no guidance. Her samples included low-level writing narrations like the following:

> A man looked an old house. He looked an old chair and proposed life. He proposed his life in the future. He entered in the room and proposed enjoying life. His hat was put off by the arrow. So he thought a strange thing. When he entered in the room, grandfather had died with the rope. He thought that he had died himself. He was very sad. (p. 53)

Ishikawa (1995) employed Homburg's definition of a T-unit, using the students' punctuation as sentence boundary markers. In analyzing the example shown above using Homburg's definition of a T-unit, the sample would include 9 sentences and 9 T-units since the sample contains no compound sentences. It also contains 11 clauses since there are two complex sentences in the passage: "When he entered in the room, grandfather had died with the rope." And "He thought that he had died himself."

However, it is more difficult to determine what should constitute an error. Should, for example, the sentence "His hat was put off by the arrow" be counted as an error free T-unit or not? Ishikawa decided to strictly define correctness: "Correctness was defined as correct with respect to discourse, vocabulary, grammar, and style, and strictly interpreted. A sentence or clause which might be correct in isolation was considered incorrect if it did not fit its discourse environment perfectly" (p. 59). According to this definition, "His hat was put off by the arrow" would be considered incorrect. She then used the following measures to determine which objective measures best discriminate low-proficiency writing samples.

Sentences per composition
T-units per composition
Error-free T-units per composition
Clauses per composition
Error-free clauses per composition
Words per composition

T-units per sentence
Error-free T-units per sentence
Clauses per sentence
Error-free clauses per sentence
Words per sentence

Error-free T-units/total T-units
Clauses per T-unit
Error-free clauses per T-unit
Words per T-unit
Words per error-free T-unit
Total words in T-units
Total words in error-free T-units

Error-free clauses/total clauses
Words per clause
Words per error-free clause
Total words in clauses
Total words in error-free clauses
Words in error-free clauses/total words in clauses (p. 60)

She found that the best measure for discriminating the syntactic maturity of the essays was the total words in error-free clauses and the second best the number of error-free clauses per composition. T-units then provide one alternative for researching the syntactic maturity of L2 student texts.

T-unit analysis, however, is not the only measure that has been used to determine writing proficiency. Grabe and Kaplan (1996) note that studies have shown that the following developmental changes can be seen in more effective L2 writing.

- increased use of adjectives
- increased nominal complexity
- increased use of free modifiers
- increased use of sentence adverbials
- increased use of relative clauses
- increased use of finite adverbial clauses
- increased use of stylistic word-order variation
- increased use of passives
- increased use of complex NP subjects
- increased range of tense and modal usage, and
- decreased use of unmodified NPs (pp. 44–45)

One recent study that looked at a variety of features of L2 texts to determine their syntactic maturity is Hinkel (2003). In her study, Hinkel undertook a quantitative analysis of 1,083 L1 and L2 academic texts to determine some of the linguistic differences that exist in L1 and L2 academic essays. As she points out, "One of the difficult issues in teaching academically bound ESL students to produce appropriate academic written text is that research has not established with certainty what specific syntactic and lexical features, when taken together, can create an impression of a seemingly simplistic or reasonably sophisticated text in written L2 discourse" (p. 275).

The purpose of her study was to identify particular grammatical and lexical features that can create an impression of textual simplicity in L2 texts as compared to L1 texts. In order to do this, based on the findings of various analyses of spoken and written corpora, she identified specific syntactic features that she believed contribute to the impression of an unsophisticated text and counted the number of times these occurred in the academic writing of L2 writers and L1 writers.

She focused specifically on the following:

(a) the frequency of the use of *be*-copula as the main verb with accompanying predicate adjective and existential *there*;

(b) vague nouns such as *guy, man, people, society, stuff, thing*;

(c) public verbs such as *acknowledge, admit, announce, assert, claim, confirm, contend, declare, disclose, insist, maintain, object, predict, protest, report, suggest*;

(d) private verbs such as *believe, consider, decide, discover, doubt, dream, esti-mate, expect, feel, find, guess, imagine, know, learn, notice, observe, pretend, reflect, think;* and

(e) expecting, tentative wanting verbs such as *attempt, desire, expect, plan, try, want.*

She found that the median frequency rate of *be*-copula and predicate adjectives of vague nouns, and of public, private, and expecting/tentative verbs was higher in L2 texts than L1 texts. Based on her findings, Hinkel maintains that L2 texts tend to include a smaller range of grammar and lexis than L1 texts and that many of the structures used in L2 texts demonstrate the use of features that are prevalent in spoken and conversational discourse.

Studies like Ishikawa (1995) and Hinkel (2003) begin to answer the questions posed by Hyland regarding the features of L2 texts and how they differ from L1 texts. Such research illustrates the kind of investigations that can be undertaken in analyzing the linguistic features of L2 writing, providing a model for small-scale classroom studies. Teachers who have students who are consistently doing poorly in L2 writing classes can examine the texts of these writers to see if they exhibit some of the lexical and grammatical features that seem to characterize simpler and less effective texts. Determining in what way the texts of particular L2 writers are more restricted in their choice of lexicon and syntactic structure provides a basis for developing a curriculum that will address these problems.

* * *

Exploring the Ideas, 3.4

The following four student essays were written in response to the prompt listed below. First, read the four essays and then holistically evaluate them by ranking them from 1 (the most effective) to 4 (the least effective). Remember with holistic assessment, the idea is to quickly read the essay and then provide an overall evaluation of the text. Then, if possible, compare your ranking with your classmates and discuss why you ranked them as you did.

Now evaluate the four student essays listed below using some type of discrete linguistic analysis to assess their syntactic maturity. You might analyze them by employing a T-unit analysis as was used in the Ishikawa (1995) study cited earlier. You could also examine the texts using the features of L2 essays that were examined in the Hinkel (2003) study, namely, the frequency of the use of *be*-copula as the main verb with accompanying predicate adjectives and existential *there*, the use of vague nouns, and public, private, and tentative wanting verbs. Then compare your results with your holistic assessment of the essay. If you find that the essays you ranked high showed minimal syntactic maturity based on some type of linguistic analysis, discuss why you ranked them highly.

PROMPT:

Most people have one possession that is especially important to them. For example, someone may value a musical instrument because of the many hours she spends playing music on it. Another person may value a piece of jewelry because it belonged to a relative. Finally, another person may value a photograph, a teapot, or a wall hanging because it reminds him of home.

Think about a possession you have that is important to you. Write a paper in which you: first describe it, and then explain why it is so important to you.

In the first part, be so specific that the reader will have a picture of it in his or her mind. In the second part, provide sufficient examples so that the reader understands exactly why the object is valuable to you (McKay, 1984, p. 56).

STUDENT A

Even though I am not the materialistic type of person and even though I don't like to use the word possession because I feel kind of a selfish person. But I have something special, it is a ring my mother gave to me around for years ago before I left my country to the U.S. for my education.

The ring is 18K gold with my initial engraved in it, it is a very small and simple ring and looks like a wedding ring.

I consider the ring important to me not because I like gold or any fancy jewelry, but because it was given to me by somebody whom I love and respect. And because every time I look at it I remember my mother, family, my country and people.

It took me a while before I adopted to the American culture, so I felt lonely and the ring was my only companion.

Everytime I look at the ring I also remember the advice my mother gave with it. She told me, "Son you are going to a country with different language and culture. You are going to face problems but be strong and struggle to get your education and come back to us."

So as you can conclude it is not the materialistic value of the ring that is important to me, it is the memory with the ring.

STUDENT B

Three years ago when I came to America, I brought a small Persian rug which was very valuable to me. It was made up by people who lived in villages in Iran. It has a rectanglar shape, containing a mixture of bright blue, white, green, red and some other colors showing the rug's picture nicely. The picture on the rug was made by some beautiful bird, flying in the sky. The material which was used for making the rug is soft and delicate. So the rug is light and too easy to carry it.

The reason I love this particular rug described above is first that was a gift from my grandmother when I was 15 years old. Since then I always took care of it. It was kept in my room all the time. I used to look at it very morning when I woke up. It was a very beautiful rug I have ever seen. When I look at it carefully I can't stop admiring all the effort and art which were applied by people who made it. Second I have another memory of my rug, I used to pray on that rug every day. That's why it is very valuable to me. Third when my grandmother died I always felt I was not alone because I have something from her to remind of her. I know it was very important to my grandmother so I try to keep and take care of it well. And I don't want to exchange it with anything else in this world.

STUDENT C

As a rule I don't keep anything that brings me memories from the past. I don't know why, but I almost always get rid of my things and replace them for new ones. Friends tell me that my places (very often) has a different look and that's because I'm constantly changing my furniture. However, there is one thing that I have kept over the years and it is a picture of a big portion of my family and relatives. This is not a big picture, it is rather small. It was taken on Mothers' Days a few years ago. There are so many people in this picture that is hard to recognize their faces. Starting from left to right you could see my four uncles, followed my mother (smiling as usual), my two sisters, who look like they have been fighting, my grandmother is right in the center of the picture, I noticed her face and it is like saying "When are you going to finish taking this picture," three of my aunts are in the right side of my grandmother. Now this is the first row, because in the second one I could see (they are in front sitting down) my fourth brothers who look like angels. (They must be up to something), my father who looks bord, my four cousins are also here. And I could see their big teeth. Everybody is in my mother's living room which looks beautiful with all those flowers given by her children. I could see the wall which had been painted recently of white they look so clean, I can not see any chairs in the living room, but in the left side (down) of the picture I could see part of the table with a big cake that looks like a wedding cake. It is too bad that the picture is a little bit too dark because you can't appreciate very well the guy in the front row sitting down on the right (guess who?*) Why do I like this picture? Because it was taken on a day that all of us were very happy, especially me. Everytime I look at this picture brings me good feelings about my people back home. This is the only picture that I have of all of them together. This is the picture of my beautiful family.

*myself

STUDENT D

I have one tennis racket that is important to me for a long time. I would like to describe my tennis racket and explain why it's important to me.

My tennis racket that I bought when I was in high school is a steel racket. The shape is everybody can imagine because I guess everybody know how a tennis racket looks like. On particular thing of my racket is it's made from steel which differs from the wood racket. The color of the racket is silver and the end of the glip has red color on which a white letter "w," which is a beginning letter of bland name, "Wilson." The red color seems that this racket belongs to female player.

The racket is very important to me because it has been teaching me something special. Since I got the racket, I have been playing a lot of games with other players. Sometime I won several games and sometimes I lost; however, everytime the racket seemed to tell me something special. I don't know what it is exactly, but I think it might be a kind of patience. It didn't matter if I won the game or not. The important thing was that I had patience while I was playing. When I was winning, I had patience to win the game. When I was defeated by the player, I had also patience to the player and myself, I think.

Of course, I brought the racket when I came to the United States. Sometimes I play tennis with my friend. Whenever I see my tennis racket, it reminds me of that I should have patience to every body with whom I'm related and everything which happens to me.

(Source of essay, McKay, 1984, pp. 57–60)

* * *

Defining Contrastive Rhetoric Analysis

While studies on the linguistic features of L2 texts offer valuable information on the differences between L1 and L2 texts, some argue that such studies are too limited in scope in that they do not address issues of genre and culture. These individuals argue instead for a contrastive rhetoric approach to text analysis.

A focus on contrastive rhetoric began with the work of Kaplan (1966). In this seminal study, Kaplan analyzed the essays of 600 L2 students from various language and cultural backgrounds in order to characterize their rhetorical development. Based on his analysis, he argued that various cultures exemplify different types of rhetorical development. According to Kaplan, writers from Arabic culture tend to exhibit parallelisms in their writing. Texts from what he terms Oriental cultures (referring to Chinese and Korean but not Japanese) tend to be marked by indirection, whereas writers from Romance language backgrounds and Russia seem to exhibit more digression in their writing. Although his study has been widely criticized for its methodology, it nevertheless provided the impetus for an examination of how rhetorical development differs according to one's linguistic and cultural background.

Connor (1996) defines contrastive rhetoric as "an area of research in second language acquisition that identifies problems in composition encountered by second language writers and, by referring to the rhetorical strategies of the first language, attempts to explain them" (p. 5). Kaplan (2001) maintains that writers from different cultures and linguistic background may differ in their answers to the following questions.

1. What may be discussed?
2. Who has the authority to speak/write? Or: Who has the authority to write to whom under what circumstance?
3. What form(s) may the writing take?
4. What is evidence?
5. What arrangement of evidence is likely to appeal (be convincing) to readers? (p. ix)

Kaplan notes that in answer to the first question, in the U.S. it might be considered appropriate to consider the issue of abortion as a topic for a class essay. However, in Northern Europe (Finland, Norway, Sweden, etc.) it would generally be considered inappropriate to assign an essay on this topic because abortion is considered exclusively a medical question. The aim of contrastive rhetoric is to find out how cultures differ in their answer to the five questions listed above.

The field has been criticized for frequently assuming that L2 writers of English should acquire the rhetorical patterns of western culture rather than using English according to their own rhetorical development. Land and Whitley (1989), for example, argue that by asking L2 writers to use the rhetorical patterns of western English-speaking cultures, "we require our

ESL students to share and reproduce in their writing our world view, one to which they are, of course alien. Such instruction is composition as colonization" (p. 289). Reid (1992), on the other hand, maintains that studies in contrastive rhetoric are not intended to suggest that certain rhetorical patterns are superior. Rather, because L2 writers are generally compared with L1 writers in western academic contexts, L2 writers themselves often consider one of their learning objectives to master the rhetorical patterns of western English-speaking countries.

Doing Contrastive Rhetoric Analysis

One of the most challenging aspects of undertaking research in contrastive rhetoric is to arrive at a productive methodology. Kaplan's (1966) method involved looking for rhetorical patterns in the texts of L2 writers from particular cultural backgrounds and then making generalizations about the rhetoric of various cultures. Yet, as Mohan and Lo (1985) point out, differences in the texts of L2 writers as compared with L1 writers could be due to L2 students' lack of proficiency in English rather than to cultural differences. Another method used in contrastive rhetoric studies is to examine the texts of proficient writers from two cultures in order to determine how writers from various cultures tend to differ in the development of a particular genre. The methodological problem that arises in such studies is to determine how to select representative authors and examples and how to compare texts from a particular genre while minimizing the effect of translation.

Another methodological approach in contrastive rhetoric studies is to examine what learners are taught about the development of particular texts in their rhetoric books, assuming that this is what the culture considers to be effective writing. Jenkins and Hinds (1987), for example, examined the models included in L1 textbooks on the writing of business letters in English, French, and Japanese in order to arrive at some rhetorical differences that exist in how students are taught to write business letters in these cultures. The problem with this approach is that what rhetoric textbooks promote as the typical rhetorical development of a particular genre may not be what in fact proficient writers from that culture use.

Another method used in contrastive rhetoric studies is to examine how the use of particular syntactic features differs cross-culturally. Hinkel (1995), for example, investigated how the use of modals of obligation (e.g., *must, have to, should, ought to* and *need to*) differs depending on one's cultural background. In order to do this, she compared the use of modals in 455 academic essays written by Chinese, Japanese, Korean, Indonesian, and Vietnamese speakers with 280 essays of native English speakers. She found that L2 and L1 texts differed in the degree to which they used these modals and the contexts in which they used them. For example, L2 texts tended to exhibit more use of modals of obligation than L1 texts in dealing with the topics of academics, family and friendship, and traditions. Cultural differences in the context in which modals are used resulted in sentences like the following.

> According to Confucianism, people *have to* respect their parents. They also *have to* respect teachers. Teachers are like parents to students and we *have to* follow their advice. (Korean) (p. 331)

> When I study here I *must* work very hard. I *must* study to respect my parents and to participate in the development of my country. (Chinese) (p. 331)

> All married couples *must* have a baby because it is their duty. However, women *must* raise their children, not babysitters. (Japanese) (p. 336)

A more recent methodological approach to contrastive rhetoric is the use of a corpus to analyze how writers from different cultures enact moves in a specific genre. This methodology is exemplified in a study by Upton and Connor (2001). The data for the study came from a larger corpora of job application letters and resumes written by business students from the U.S., Belgium, Finland, Germany, and Thailand. In their analysis the authors used a coding system for analyzing the moves of a letter of application based on an earlier study. These moves are as follows.

1. Identify the source of information. (Explain how and where you learned of the position.)
2. Apply for the position. (State desire for consideration.)
3. Provide argument, including supporting information, for the job application.
   a. Implicit argument based on neutral evidence or information about background and experience.
   b. Arguments based on what would be good for the hiring company. ("My intercultural training will be an asset to your international negotiations team.")
   c. Arguments based on what would be good for the applicant. ("This job will give me the opportunity to test my intercultural training.")
4. Indicate desire for an interview or a desire for future contact, or specify means of further communication/how to be contacted.
5. Express politeness (pleasantries) or appreciation at the end of the letter.
6. Offer to provide more information.
7. Reference attached resume. (p. 318)

The data on which this study is based consisted of 70 letters of application written by Belgians, 26 letters written by Finns, and 57 letters written by

Americans. All of the students were undergraduate university students who were taking a business writing course. Upton and Connor coded each of these letters according to the rhetorical moves listed above. They then looked at the politeness strategies the writers used in enacting these moves. They found that the Americans in their study tended to be much more patterned, almost formulaic in their use of politeness strategies. The Belgians, on the other hand, tended to be much more individual in their expression of politeness with the Finns falling in between. For example, in enacting move 4 (indicating a desire for an interview or future contact), a representative example from an American student was:

> When reviewing your list of candidates for this position, please consider me for an interview. (p. 320)

On the other hand, a representative example from a Belgian or Finn would be:

> I would very much appreciate having an interview with you during which I can prove my English communication skills. (p. 320)

There are several features of the methodology used in this study that are significant in regard to contrastive rhetoric studies. First, the study made use of a corpus to analyze specific moves and politeness formulae. Second, the corpus included data from a specific genre, in this case letters of application. And finally, the study clearly specified the cultural background of the writers and the context in which they were writing the letters. This type of analysis allows for a much more fine tuned analysis of cultural differences than was present in the early contrastive rhetoric investigations.

Reviewing studies in contrastive rhetoric and examining the methods they use has several benefits. First, doing so may be of value to you in designing your own contrastive rhetoric study. Second, becoming familiar with the findings of contrastive rhetoric studies can help you design materials that raise learners' awareness of how rhetorical patterns differ cross-culturally. Finally, an awareness of the findings of contrastive rhetoric studies is useful in the assessment of L2 texts so that assessors do not penalize L2 writers for the use of rhetorical patterns that differ from their own.

* * *

Exploring the Ideas, 3.5

Read one of the contrastive rhetoric studies listed below and then answer the questions that follow. If you are familiar with another contractive rhetoric study, you can analyze this article instead.

Articles:

Ferris, D. (1994). Rhetorical strategies in student persuasive writing: Differences between native and non-native English speakers. *Research in the Teaching of English, 28*(1), 45–65. (This study analyzes 60 persuasive texts written by L1 and L2 university students to determine how they differ on 33 variables.)

Hinkel, E. (2004). Tense, aspect and the passive voice in L1 and L2 academic texts. *Language Teaching Research, 8*(1), 5–29. (This study analyzes placement and diagnostic tests written by L1 and L2 speakers to determine how these texts differ in the use of past, present and future tenses, the progressive and perfect aspects, and passive verbs.)

Scarcella, R. (1984). How writers orient their readers in expository essays: A comparative study of native and non-native English writers. *TESOL Quarterly, 18*(4), 671–689. (This study analyzes 110 essays written by native and non-native English speakers to determine what linguistic devices they use to engage their readers.)

Questions:

1. What was the focus of the study?
2. What written data were examined in the study?
3. How were the data collected?
4. How were the data analyzed?
5. Is there any additional information you would like to have on the methodology of the study?
6. What were the findings of the study? Do they seem justified in light of the evidence presented in the study?
7. What were the pedagogical implications of the study? Do they seem warranted in the context of the study?

Be prepared to share your assessment of the research report with your classmates.

* * *

Text Analysis of Teacher Texts

Doing Text Analysis of Teacher Feedback

The benefits of teacher feedback on student essays have been widely debated, with some questioning its value. Frequently the criticism of teacher feedback arises from the belief that teacher comments are vague and confusing to students. (See, for example, Zamel, 1985.) Clearly any study of the effectiveness of teacher comments depends on the ability to categorize the type of feedback that teachers give students and to assess the effect of such feedback on the development of students' writing.

One study that attempts to do this is Ferris (1997). In this study, Ferris examined over 1,600 marginal and end comments written by teachers on 110 drafts of student essays written by 47 advanced L2 students. She then analyzed the length of the written feedback, the type of comments made, the use of hedges, and whether or not the comments were text specific. In reference to the type of comments teachers wrote, she developed the following categories.

1. Ask for information/question
   Did you work out this problem with your roommates?
2. Make a request/question
   Can you provide a thesis statement here—What did you learn from this?
3. Make a request/statement
   This paragraph might be better earlier in the essay.
4. Make a request/imperative
   Mention what Zinsser says about parental pressure.
5. Give information/question
   Most states do allow a waiting period before an adoption is final—Do you feel that all such laws are wrong?
6. Give information/statement
   Iowa law favors parental rights. Michigan and California consider the best interests of the child.
7. Make a positive comment/statement or exclamation
   A nice start to your essay! You've done an impressive job of finding facts and quotes to support your argument.
8. Make a grammar/mechanics comment/question/statement or imperative
   Past or present tense?
   a. *Your verb tenses are confusing me in this paragraph.*
   b. *Don't forget to spell-check!* (p. 321)

Ferris then assessed the impact of these comments on student revisions. She developed a subjective rating scale based on the degree to which students utilized the comments to revise their essays by making no attempt, a minimal attempt, or a substantive attempt to address the comment. She also analyzed the changes students made to determine whether or not they improved the paper, had mixed effects, or negligible or negative effects on the essay. Overall she found that the changes students made in response to teachers' comments tended to improve the students' papers and that marginal requests for information, requests (regardless of their grammatical form), and summary comments on grammar led to the most substantive changes. Ferris's typology is based on teachers' responses to the writing of advanced L2 students. It may well be that a different coding system would be needed for less advanced students.

Ferris's study illustrates one type of research that can be undertaken regarding teacher feedback on student essays. Supplementing this research could be research on determining students' preferences for the various types of feedback. In addition, verbal reports could be used to determine how students go about processing the feedback provided by teachers.

*   *   *

Exploring the Ideas, 3.6

Listed below are three essays written by intermediate-level L2 university students. To begin, respond to the essays as if you were the teacher of the students' L2 writing class. Make any marginal or end comments that you believe would help students in revising their essays.

Now examine your comments using the Ferris (1997) coding system included in the chapter. Note any comments that you find difficult to categorize. If you were using this system in a research project and had these problems of categorization, how would you deal with them?

PROMPT:

Write a two-paragraph essay developed as follows:

First paragraph: Describe a particular place in which you feel comfortable. It can be a corner in your room, a street in your neighborhood, or a place in the country or at the beach. Try to make each detail of your description contribute to a clear picture of this place.

Second paragraph: Explain why this place is "comfortable." You may use additional examples to illustrate your definition. (McKay, 1984, p. 154)

STUDENT A

Repulse Bay is the only place in which I would spend my whole life without hesitation. It is located in the southern part of the Hong Kong Island. The beach which is half-moon shape, is deeply covered by fair and smooth sand. The water is blue in color, with unusually good smell of fresh sea water which no other beach can give me. The scenery is picturesque. There are some very extraordinary rocks which eject out from the steep sea-cliffs, forming some natural scrupturers. Laying on the golden sand, soothing by the warm sun and soft-breeze, and embracing by the graceful scrupturers wash away my worried, miseries, and strains completely.

I enjoy staying in a place where social tension and pollution do not exist. It has to be natural, gigantic and extraordinary. I prefer ocean scene rather than mountain view because the former is always the representation and symbol of softness and motherhood. It should also be quiet and impressive because I enjoy privacy very much. No other place can give me such comfort and fulfillment, but my most favorite beach—Repulse Bay.

STUDENT B

A particular place where I would feel comfortable would be a peaceful place. A place where I could only hear the birds sing. A place where I could feel the wind blowing my hair. A place that has beautiful green grass, and some of my favorite flowers, for example; red roses, red carnations, and yellow daisies. This place should also have different kinds of miniature fruit trees. for example; an apple tree, a cherry tree, and an orange tree.

The particular place where I always like to be is in my mother's garden. I feel very comfortable and happy when I'm there. I do my homework there, because I feel I can concentrate more than when I'm inside the house. The garden for me is so special, because I can really notice nature. The smell of the flowers and the growing of the fruits make me go everyday and stay there for at least an hour.

STUDENT C

The left corner of my room, just opposite my bed, is the most comfortable place for me. A brown modern-designed desk, which is placed close to the wall, is matched with an orange armchair. Just above the desk on the wall is hung with a small abstract painting. On the right, between the desk and the window, there is a stand lamp. On the other side of the desk is the brown wooden bookshelves. It stands from the floor up to the ceiling. Piles of books are put in it according to alphabetical order of author.

This place is comfortable because it is quiet and elegant. Sitting on the chair and looking out through the window, it is the nice backyard which is cultivated with colorful charming flowers. People scarcely go down the backyard, that I can read my books quietly with any border. If I am not reading, I can switch on the cassette on my desk and listen to the music. This corner is so lovely that I always spend a whole night in it.

(Source of essays, McKay, 1984, pp. 156–157)

Doing Text Analysis of Teacher Designed Classroom Materials

Teachers develop a variety of texts to be used in the classroom including course outlines, prompts for student essays, classroom activities, and exam questions. Studies on these texts can help teachers become more aware of the patterns in their own texts and provide a basis for familiarizing students with the typical patterns in teacher texts. One example of such research is Horowitz's (1986) study of essay examination prompts. In the study, Horowitz collected 284 essay examination prompts from 15 academic departments. Based on his analysis of these prompts he arrived at a typology of the following four purposes that exam questions may serve:

1. Display familiarity with a concept.
2. Display familiarity with the relation between/among concepts.
3. Display familiarity with a process.
4. Display familiarity with argumentation. (p. 110)

He then provided examples of each category based on the data he gathered. He argued that familiarizing students with such a typology and offering examples of each type would better prepare students to write essay exams.

The value of such research is that it raises teachers' awareness of the features of specific pedagogical genres, in this case, essay examination prompts. Given such typologies, teachers can then investigate students' preferences regarding particular kinds of prompts; they can also examine which type of prompt results in the most developed student essays. Clearly far more research is needed into pedagogical genres, like essay prompts and teacher designed classroom tasks. One of the difficulties in undertaking such research is to gather a large enough sample to be able to make generalizations about the common moves that characterize a particular type of teacher-designed materials.

Text Analysis of Second Language Teaching Materials

Certainly one of the most pervasive and influential types of classroom materials is textbooks. In our discussion of textbooks we focus on two ways of researching textbooks. One is to focus on the language used in the textbook—the grammatical structures and lexicon and their use in dialogues and reading texts. The second is to research the social information in the textbooks in terms of such features as the gender, economic class, and ethnic background of the characters. One of the best ways to research the language of textbooks is to use a corpus. In order to demonstrate how this can be done, we begin with a discussion of corpus-based research.

Defining Corpus-Based Research

A *corpus* is a collection of written or spoken naturally occurring language that is stored electronically. Corpora are of two general types. The first is a *specialized corpus* that contains texts of a particular type such as medical discourse, L2 learner language, or literary works. A *general corpus*, on the other hand, includes a wide range of text types, including written and spoken texts, as well as texts of different registers or fields.

Several factors affect the design of a corpus, among them the following (Hunston, 2002).

- *Size*—With the increasing data storage capability of computers, it is possible to collect larger and larger corpora. Some argue that too much data in a corpus can be overwhelming, and thus, they support the use of a more limited corpus. In general, the size of a corpus is related to the purpose of the research. For lexicographers, having a very large corpus is helpful. On the other hand, if one wishes to examine the language used in a particular type of genre, such as academic textbooks, a more limited corpus can be quite valuable.

- *Content*—The content of a corpus should be suited to the purpose of the research. As Hunston (2002) points out, "a corpus is neither good nor bad in itself, but suited or not suited to a particular purpose" (p. 26). For example, if a researcher wants to determine the authenticity of informal spoken dialogues in an L2 textbook, two corpora are needed: one containing textbook dialogues and the other a corpora of spoken informal conversations.

- *Representativeness*—If the purpose of the research is to examine general spoken informal conversational English, then the corpus should include conversations that demonstrate variation in the gender and age of the speakers, as well as diversity in the situations used.

- *Permanence*—If a corpus is to remain effective, it must be consistently updated to reflect changes in the language.

One of the main advantages of using a corpus is that it provides information that is more reliable than native speaker intuition. As Biber and Conrad (2001) note, one common intuition about language use is that the present progressive is the unmarked or most frequent choice in informal conversation. Yet their research demonstrates that in fact the simple present tense is the unmarked choice in conversation. There are, however, limitations to corpus-based research. For one thing, a corpus can show only what is included in the corpus so that "a statement about evidence in a corpus is a statement about that corpus, not about the language or register of which the corpus is a sample. Thus conclusions about language drawn from a corpus have to be treated as deductions, not as facts" (Hunston, 2002, p. 23). The most serious drawback of corpus-based research, however, is that it presents language out of context. Hence, the researcher generally knows little about who made the statement, in what context, and with what intent and paralinguistic features.

Corpus-based research includes a variety of specialized terminology. For example, in corpus research, *tokens* are the number of running words in a corpus, whereas *types* are the number of different words in the corpus. In a beginning level textbook, where an effort is made to recycle new vocabulary, one could anticipate fewer types than would appear in advanced level materials. *Lemmas* are composed of words with related forms such as *go, goes,* and *went.* Finally *tagging* refers to the addition of a code on words in a corpus. A *tagger,* for example, would allow a researcher to retrieve only the noun form of *help.* (For further reading on corpus linguistics terminology and research approaches, as well as useful Web sites, see the book review section of *TESOL Quarterly, 37,* 2.)

Doing Corpus-Based Research

Two areas of corpus-based research are especially valuable for developing and assessing L2 textbooks. The first is the calculation of *word frequency lists.* A frequency list is simply a list of all the types of words that appear in a corpus, along with the number of occurrences of each word.

Let us take, for example, the appearance of common verbs in English. Based on the research of Biber et al. (1999) with the *Longman Grammar of Spoken and Written English,* Biber and Conrad (2001) point out that nearly 400 different verbs occur over 20 times per million words. However, only 63 verbs occur more than 500 times and only 12 verbs occur more than 1,000 times. These 12 verbs are: *say, get, go, know, think, see, make, come, take, want, give,* and *mean.* With this information, L2 textbook writers would clearly want to include the 12 most common verbs in beginning level materials.

Word frequency lists are even more useful when they are sorted by register. For example, whereas the 12 most common verbs are very important in conversation where they account for over 45% of all verbs, they account for only 11% of verbs in academic prose. This kind of information is especially helpful in designing materials for English for Specific Purposes. For example, knowing what are the most frequently used verbs in a corpus of business texts would be valuable information in designing English for Business textbooks.

A second type of analysis that can be done with a corpus is *concordancing.* Concordancing programs allow the user to bring together all the instances of a particular word along with the words that surround it. The selected word is referred to as the *node word/phrase.* For example, the following is a partial list of the use of word *disclose* as it appears in the Brown corpus of written English sorted by the word that follows on the right. Presenting *disclose* sorted right as shown here demonstrates that *disclose* often collocates or goes with the word *details.* On the other hand, if the list were sorted by the word on the left, a researcher would be better able to make generalization about the use of *disclose* as an infinitive. The best way to read concordance lines is to skim them initially from top to bottom, looking for central patterns.

```
Concordances for disclose = 70        Net Dictionary entries for disclose
1     s as often  neglect as hesitance to disclose. A busy president,  conversant with
2       ``While it may be appropriate to disclose an item of official  information und
3      his firm.  However, he  refused to disclose any further details about Mr Chan.
4     se  material that it was obliged to disclose anyway.  Mr  Kalisher was later brie
5     ng's request for the  Government to disclose at today's Legco meeting recent  dip
6     Mr Tony Eason, said the proposal to disclose Category  II buildings did not match
7      consequences.  Few were willing to disclose details of  the meeting. The Liberal
8     on the Prince of Wales Hospital to  disclose details of an internal investigation
9      police last Sunday but refused to  disclose details of the arrest.  Mr Huang sai
10    er examination.  Mr Lam declined to disclose details of the incident, saying an
11    sisted  yesterday that it would not disclose details of the PM's diary  so far in
12    compense, and has asked Barclays to disclose documents relevant to its claim.
13    as exceeding $10,000,000 (we  don't disclose financial figures to the public). It
14    ess,'' said Ms Yiu, who declined to disclose her full  name.  Many food operators
15    A  dismayed Mr Tsang, who would not disclose his full name, said  government poli
16    d so  simple that he didn't like to disclose his ignorance.     While Mr& Blatz w
17     For the first time, companies must disclose in a clear and concise manner how
18    ted to Britain, is   threatening to disclose in his memoirs this year.        So
19       said it would be inappropriate to disclose information on  import and export de
20    recorded the conversation and would disclose it to their  families and schools.
21    ecorded the  conversation and would disclose it to their families and  schools.
```

The data listed above and used below in *Exploring the Ideas, 3.7* was taken from the Brown corpus. The Brown corpus was compiled in 1961 and includes 500 samples of over 2,000 words each. The samples represent a wide range of styles and varieties of prose. The searches were taken from the Web Concordancer that is available free on the Web at http://www.edict. com.hk/concordance.

*   *   *

Exploring the Ideas, 3.7

The verbs *declare, disclose,* and *expose* all have the feature *to state*; however, they differ in their syntactic patterns and collocations. Examine the following concordances of these three verbs from the Brown corpus. To begin, identify what words each verb tends to collocate with. For example, the previous data suggests that the verb *disclose* often collates with the word *detail.* Second, look for the common syntactic patterns used with each verb. Do some of these verbs tend to be used more widely in the passive or infinitive form? Finally, formulate any tentative conclusions you could make about the difference in the collocation and syntactic patterns of these three verbs.

You will notice that the entry for *expose* contains both the noun and verb form. If you were using this list for research purposes, it would be wise to use a tagger to elicit only the verb form.

```
Concordances for declare = 41 Net Dictionary entries for declare
1    s' fly the pro-democracy banner and declare a  fully-elected legislature as the
2    rupting, but refused his request to declare a ceasefire for Russian   Christmas,
3     would have to call in the army and declare a state of emergency if   the disput
4    nds they received.   Members should declare all interests they received directly
5    said his motion called on  China to declare an amnesty and release all political
6    cing a mechanism for the courts to  declare an election void and streamlining so
7    h surplus now that we think we  can declare another dividend,'' Mr Etches said.
8    GISLATIVE Councillors will  have to declare any sponsorship or material benefits
9     in July, then I  would not need to declare anything.''  The Legislative  Counci
10   d,'' Mr Etches said.  ``We  hope to declare at least one more dividend between M
11   >  (92:07:29>  (3>  Councillors to  declare donations  By LANA  WONG and CONNIE
12   rlier that members did not have to  declare donations from their political organ
13   t that legislators  did not have to declare donations received by their parties,
14    servant Exco members had little to declare except  their posts in the Governmen
15   Anson Chan Fang On-sang, has yet to declare her  interests.   (2197>  (92:07:28>
16   Smith: "Of course,   Rhodesia could declare herself independent, and she would b
17   nd May. While he is not expected to declare his formal candidature for at leas
18       MICHAEL ATHERTON'S decision to declare in Sydney yesterday with   Graeme Hi
19   lines, councillors are  required to declare land and property of ``substantial v
20   entury.        As a Yorkshireman, I declare my interest. I await the call from
21    stands before the congregation  to declare publicly their faith and to be recei
22   and  thereafter a hundred followers declare secrecy a higher  verity. This is si
23   ian conscience was leading  some to declare slavery wrong and to act accordingly
24   c, say the only two legislators to  declare such directorships.  Mr Peter Wong H
25   rgotten hearing  his adored Czarina declare that all truly great men  had odditi
26    next year unless the President can declare that it is safe for them to return
27   Year's Eve address to the nation to declare that it was his "constitutional du
28   ldings.  He  had earlier refused to declare that the title to a flat below  the
29   plaintiffs are asking the  court to declare that they can buy flats in the Jing
30   d, "it  is no longer fashionable to declare that we can say  nothing certain abo
31   ically, to draw a line here  and to declare that, in due course, this Council wi
32   ent financial advisers will have to declare the  commission they will earn. The
33   ndlord, Mr Lau Wong-fat, need  only declare the country of their holdings, which
34   ey note,  the Revenue Service might declare the pension plan  is discriminatory
35   . The Milan stock exchange had to   declare the trades null and void to avoid fo
36   Legislative Councillors failed to   declare their affiliation to political group
37    are  required by the Government to declare their interests.   Earlier this year
38   and the company was quickly able to declare very liberal dividends on its capit
```

39   r properties. But Mr Ngai did not declare where his properties were, saying he
40   expected its staff to voluntarily declare whether they had the right of abode
41   y-five years of married life could declare with some pride that her husband had

Concordances for **expose** = 23 Net Dictionary entries for expose
1   ROVER, the first car maker to expose a 1995 model, has given the Metro
2   nsurance and investments. This will expose,and therefore end, some shady pra
3   plaster on the walls hacked off to expose bare   brick, the ceiling strung wit
4   ime Minister is absolutely right to expose it as a   serious threat to the futu
5   Recently,   WWRL won praise for its expose of particular cases of employment a
6   id the release of the tapes   would expose other underground activists, in effe
7   o pulled his jacket to one side to expose part of an imitation pistol he was c
8   resent, the truth we are trying to expose,right now, is that the makers of c
9   ve gone undercover as passengers to expose rogue   minicab drivers and pass inf
10   y to manipulate their profits. This expose so enraged some companies and the
11   ling report meant that we could not expose the   children and staff to the risk
12   -Semitism than this opportunity to expose the exact link between the respectab
13   phase   of the Tories' campaign to expose the fault-lines in the opposition's
14   t would, according to the minutes, "expose the government to serious   criticis
15   and the existing MTRC operation to expose the problems implicit in the existin
16   on). I consider it to be my job to expose the public to what is being written
17   tent. ## BUT IF THE Trial did not expose the special Nazi mania so deadly to
18   y answers during the past year   to expose the spending of some $1 million on p
19   ldwide product domestically   could expose the supposed barrier between interna
20   ally amendment- an act which could expose the United States to no practical ri
21   strategy of the South has been to expose the vices of the North, to demonstr
22   d him because they feared he might expose their secrets and corrupt practice.
23   nounced a new activity designed to expose thousands of teen-age boys and girl

Concordances for **disclose** = 70   Net Dictionary entries for disclose
1   s as often neglect as hesitance to disclose. A busy president, conversant with
2   ``While it may be appropriate to disclose an item of official information und
3   his firm. However, he refused to disclose any further details about Mr Chan.
4   se material that it was obliged to disclose anyway. Mr Kalisher was later brie
5   ng's request for the Government to disclose at today's Legco meeting recent dip
6   Mr Tony Eason, said the proposal to disclose Category II buildings did not match
7   consequences. Few were willing to disclose details of the meeting. The Liberal
8   on the Prince of Wales Hospital to disclose details of an internal investigation
9   police last Sunday but refused to disclose details of the arrest. Mr Huang sai
10   er examination. Mr Lam declined to disclose details of the incident, saying an
11   sisted yesterday that it would not disclose details of the PM's diary so far in
12   compense, and has asked Barclays to disclose documents relevant to its claim.
13   as exceeding $10,000,000 (we don't disclose financial figures to the public). It

14   ess,'' said Ms Yiu, who declined to <u>disclose</u> her full name. Many food operators

15   A dismayed Mr Tsang, who would not <u>disclose</u> his full name, said government poli

16   d so simple that he didn't like to <u>disclose</u> his ignorance.   While Mr& Blatz w

17   For the first time, companies must <u>disclose</u> in a clear and concise manner how

18   ted to Britain, is   threatening to <u>disclose</u> in his memoirs this year.   So

19   said it would be inappropriate to <u>disclose</u> information on import and export de

20   recorded the conversation and would <u>disclose</u> it to their families and schools.

21   ecorded the conversation and would <u>disclose</u> it to their families and schools.

22   endently managed pension fund. To <u>disclose</u> its assets which must not be dispos

23   So far, the OECD has refused to <u>disclose</u> its country-by-country   studies, al

24   return for the defence agreeing to <u>disclose</u> material that it was obliged to dis

25   illors to decide whether or not to <u>disclose</u> more than required, it said.   On th

26   Although the Government has yet to <u>disclose</u> Mr Deng's itinerary, sources said

27   I felt it would be inopportune to <u>disclose</u> my presence. Not that I intentionall

28   e. The act makes it an offence to <u>disclose</u> official information in areas relate

29   argument that it could be unwise to <u>disclose</u> one's financial   position to a stra

30   eau of Investigation reports might <u>disclose</u>.Section 6 (j) of the Act, as w

31   plete listing and description would <u>disclose</u>.Several were born in the early dec

32   us rates, with others   expected to <u>disclose</u> similar setbacks. Mike Urmston, the

33   eeks said.   However, he refused to <u>disclose</u> specific steps for the $9 billion s

34   idelines, councillors will have to <u>disclose</u> such sponsorships or material benef

35   s at Coventry last month will today <u>disclose</u> that the   altimeters were correctly

36   o invest. The guidance notes also <u>disclose</u> that the new operators will get a s

37   Frank Young, she stopped the cab to <u>disclose</u> that Young had been shot dead, tear

38   s, Mr Tam urged both governments to <u>disclose</u> the contents of the negotiations.

39   sed the Government's willingness to <u>disclose</u> the list. But the Secretary for Pl

40   eration. The spokesman declined to <u>disclose</u> the other plans but said the board

41   nes will not require councillors to <u>disclose</u> the specific amount of the financia

42   the councillors are not required to <u>disclose</u> the amount of benefits they receive

43   ar, forcing   financial salesmen to <u>disclose</u> the amount of their commission, may

44   irport issue but said he could not <u>disclose</u> the contents of the plan. The Chine

45   is not going to be our practice to <u>disclose</u> the details of our relationships wi

46   thout requiring the councillors to <u>disclose</u> the exact amount of sponsorships or

47   compensation.   The failure to <u>disclose</u> the findings of a City tribunal whic

48   m''. He said it would be wrong to <u>disclose</u> the information to a third party wit

49   s Li said. The   bureau refused to <u>disclose</u> the location of the hotel or how   l

50   nics boss Mr Gulu Lalvani would not <u>disclose</u> the name of the buyer of his Cheste

51   tters and fishermen. He refused to <u>disclose</u> the name of the developer. A total

52   kong, Mr Lalvani said he could not <u>disclose</u> the name of the new owner but would

53   prepared to ask the Government to <u>disclose</u> the relevant exchanges between Brit

54   ance, it may not be appropriate to <u>disclose</u> the same item of information under a

55   tions to parties requiring them to <u>disclose</u> the source of funds they received.

56   nt, asked that Osman be ordered to <u>disclose</u> the source of his funding because he

57   ndings and urged the government to <u>disclose</u> the survey methods. An Agriculture

58   House, Causeway Bay. They did not <u>disclose</u> the time or the number of participa

```
59   ars to    complete. NatWest will not disclose the total cost, but the final bill i
60   f Article  /2, of the Agreement, to disclose the use thereof in  the projects and
61   over sales staff being forced to   disclose their commissions and charges contin
62   banks and the Bank of   England to disclose their customers' identities, claimin
63   be   released soon but declined to disclose their identities.   The three bisho
64   s improvement if companies   had to disclose their positions fully, and executive
65   ad until their speeches  refused to disclose their stance on the electoral   arran
66   ad until their  speeches refused to disclose their stance on the electoral   arran
67   ad until  their speeches refused to disclose their stance on the   electoral arran
68   valry east of the  Macon railway to disclose to Sherman that he was missing   the
69   was fair.  His lawyers  refused to disclose what the costs were.  It is believed
70   the Government is  in a position to disclose whatever it feels fit while the Exco
```

* * *

Exploring the Ideas, 3.8

Listed below are the Web sites for some free corpora with concordancers. Identify a lexical pattern that you want to research. For example, you might undertake research on the use of *interested in* versus *interesting*, or you might look for the words that collocate with a particular group of verbs that share a common meaning such as the verbs in *Exploring the Ideas, 3.7*. Then visit at least two of the Web sites and undertake a search for the problem you have identified. Be certain to note what type of data are included in the corpus you search since, as was pointed out earlier, what is included in a corpus has a significant impact on what is found. Be prepared to describe the findings of your search. (My thanks to Erkan Karabacak, a graduate student at San Francisco State University, for supplying these sites.) For additional concordancing programs see O'Keeffe and Farr (2003).

Some Online Free Corpora in English with Concordancers

The Compleat Lexical Tutor

http://132.208.224.131/

This is a very interactive Web site with various corpora. Moreover you can use your own text as a corpus in order to analyze it. It also includes many ideas for teachers and learners on how to use a corpus in class for research-based learning.

Online KWIC Concordancer

http://ysomeya.hp.infoseek.co.jp/

This site has a helpful one-million-word corpus of business letters.

MICASE (Michigan Corpus of Academic Spoken English)

http://www.hti.umich.edu/m/micase/

This site includes a 1,848,364 word transcript from 152 different texts. You can search for phrases in specified contexts. You can easily track the concordance results with references to files, full utterances, and speakers.

Web Concordancer

http://www.edict.com.hk/concordance/

This site has several corpora, including literature. This site also offers easy-to-use concordancing software for free.

British National Corpus

http://sara.natcorp.ox.ac.uk/lookup.html

This site has 100 million words of written and spoken corpus. It has easy-to-use instructions. However, key words in context are not aligned, which makes it harder to see the pattern of the context.

Collins Cobuild Corpus Concordance Sampler

http://www.collinswordbanks.co.uk/

This easy to use 56 million-word corpus has three sub corpora from Britain and the United States. It also has a short easy-to-follow guide.

Turbo Lingo

http://main.amu.edu.pl/~sipkadan/lingo.htm

This is an easy to use online concordancer in which you can paste and analyze your own corpus. It also finds two-word phrases in a corpus, which might be helpful in detecting over-used phrases in learner corpora.

WebCorp

http://www.webcorp.org.uk/

This very clever concordancer uses the whole WWW as a corpus. You also have access to the text of the key word in the concordance.

WebCONC

http://www.niederlandistik.fu-berlin.de/cgi-bin/web-conc.cgi?art=google&sprache=en

This online software does key words in context with many languages.

*   *   *

Corpus-Based Research of L2 Teaching Materials

Liu's (2003) corpus-based research focused on American English idiom teaching materials. In the study, Liu used three corpora—a corpus of spoken *professional* American English, a corpus of spoken American *media* language, and a corpus of *academic* spoken English. In this way the corpus included a wide range of spoken English registers. His next step was to identify the idioms he would search in his corpora. In order to do this, he consulted major contemporary English idiom dictionaries and phrasal verb dictionaries and selected 9,683 idioms to search.

He then searched for these idioms and tabulated their frequency in four different corpora. One of them was based on all three corpora and the other three from each of the three corpora included in his study. Based on his analysis he found that, in general, idioms were rarely used in the corpora. Furthermore, idioms are sensitive to register so that, for example, the idiom *to hang out (with)* had only 8 tokens in the professional spoken corpus with far more in the other corpora. Finally, he found that idioms can vary in form so that the meaning of the idiom *ballpark figure* was extended to *ballpark idea.*

Liu then compared the findings of his research with the information in the dictionaries he had initially consulted. What he found was that the selection of idioms in these books was inconsistent, with some of the dictionaries not including idioms that frequently appeared in the corpora he used. More importantly, the primary meaning listed for some of the idioms in the dictionaries was not consistent with those found in the corpora. For example, the primary meaning of the idiom *bring up* in the idiom dictionaries was listed as *to rear* or *educate a person (often a child)* rather than the primary meaning in the corpora *to mention* and *start discussion of an issue.* He concludes by arguing that idioms presented in teaching and reference materials "need to be selected in a more rigorous, systematic way, and should be based on authentic language rather than intuition in order to increase their content representativeness" (p. 687).

* * *

Exploring the Ideas, 3.9

Read one of the corpus-based L2 text studies listed below and then answer the questions that follow. If you are familiar with another corpus-based study that focuses on L2 written texts, you can analyze this article instead. Notice from the articles listed how corpus-based studies are being used to examine students' texts, classroom materials, and academic vocabulary.

Articles:

Coxhead, A. (2000). A new academic word list. *TESOL Quarterly, 34*(2), 213–238. (This study describes the development and evaluation of a new word list of academic vocabulary that clarifies which academic words are widely used.)

Flowerdew, L. (2003). A combined corpus and systemic-functional analysis of the problem-solution pattern in a student and professional corpus of technical writing. *TESOL Quarterly, 37*(3), 489–512. (Using a corpus of undergraduate student writing and one containing professional writing, the author describes the similarities and differences between expert and novice writing in the problem-solution pattern.)

Frazier, S. (2003). A corpus analysis of *would*-clauses without adjacent *if*-clauses. *TESOL Quarterly, 37*(3), 443–466. (This study compares how *would*-clauses without adjacent *if*-clauses are dealt with in ESL/EFL textbooks, as opposed to how they appear in three corpora.)

Questions:

1. What was the goal of the study?
2. What corpora were used?
3. What procedures were followed?
4. What were the findings of the study? Do they seem justified in light of the evidence presented?
5. What pedagogical implications were drawn? Do they seem warranted in view of the findings of the study?

Non-Corpus Research of L2 Teaching Materials

Studies of L2 teaching materials, of course, can also be done without corpora analysis. One example of this type of research is Gilmore (2004). In this study, Gilmore assessed the authenticity of dialogues in seven L2 textbooks. Gilmore chose to focus specifically on service encounters, such as a tourist asking for help at a tourist center, because they can be easily replicated outside of a classroom. In addition, the speakers are strangers so the relationship is clear. To begin, he selected service encounters that appeared in his textbook sample. The questions in the service encounter were then reformulated and used as a basis for him to undertake a similar authentic encounter outside of the classroom. These encounters were recorded and transcribed so that Gilmore could compare the discourse features of the textbook dialogues and his encounters outside of the classroom.

Nine separate discourse features were identified and compared in the two versions. These included lexical density, false starts, repetition, pauses, terminal overlap, latching, hesitation devices, and back-channels. He found considerable differences in the use of these features between the two contexts. Although he found that in some newer textbooks there were more of the discourse features found in the authentic data, he maintains that textbooks still need to present more authentic interactions in order to prepare students for their encounters outside of the classroom.

Critical Text Analysis Research

Critical text analysis, like critical discourse analysis, seeks to examine how the larger social and political framework influences what is said in a classroom. One of the early studies of this type of textbook analysis is Auerbach (1986), who examined the theoretical assumptions and social implications of curricula used in competency-based ESL programs. In the study, she argues that competency-based adult education (CBAE) materials reflect a tradition of socializing immigrants for specific roles in the existing social order. She maintains that "current CBAE/ESL texts seem to follow the tradition of preparing students to fulfill employers' needs. Many mention only minimum-wage jobs as options for newcomers—for example, busboy, maid, janitor, and factory worker—and teaches language functions of subservience, such as apologizing and following orders" (p. 418). As support for this contention, she analyzed the content of CBAE/ESL texts, citing the following dialogue from Walsh (1984) as an illustration of how the content of a dialogue can socialize immigrants for particular roles.

1. Go to work on time. Don't be late . . .
2. Work hard. Don't be lazy.
3. Work carefully. Always do your best.
4. Ask questions if you don't understand or are not sure . . .
5. Be friendly. Get along with everybody. Be nice to other workers. . . . Smile at them. Be clean and neat. (p. 418)

Another example of a study that critically examined the content of L2 textbooks is Matsuda (2002). The purpose of this study was to explore the representation of English speakers in EFL textbooks used in the first year of junior high school in Japan. Her sample included all of the 7th grade textbooks that were approved by the Monbusho (the Ministry of Education). To begin, she examined the kinds of people that were represented as English-users in Japanese EFL textbooks. In order to explore this question, she identified the nationality of the main characters introduced in the early sections of each textbook before the regular chapters began and counted the number of words uttered by each character. She found that the majority of the main characters in the textbooks were from Japan (34) or inner circle countries (e.g., the U.S., Canada, and Australia) (30). The number of characters from other countries was quite limited (8). In addition she found that speakers from inner circle countries, although lower in number than Japanese characters, spoke considerably more words (3,074 as compared to 2,844). Furthermore, characters from other countries spoke hardly at all. The high number of speakers from inner circle countries, coupled with the number of words spoken by these characters, suggests that the owners and main users of English are native speakers. Little recognition is given in the text to the increasing use of English as a lingua franca for bilingual speakers of English. Studies such as this one illustrate how simply counting the country of origin of characters in a textbook, along with the number of words spoken by these characters, can be used to discover some of the social assumptions being made in a textbook.

Another study of the social assumptions contained in L2 textbooks is a study by Iwasaki (2000), which examined the cultural context and content of Japanese high school oral communication textbooks. In her investigation of twelve Ministry of Education approved oral communication textbooks, Iwasaki sought to determine if the dialogues used characters and topics from what Cortazzi and Jin (1999) call the *source culture* (i.e., Japan) the *target culture* (i.e., native English-speaking cultures) or the *international target culture* (i.e., interactions between L2 speakers of English). She found that the source culture was used in 83% of the interactions and that in 60% of the textbooks the source culture was used exclusively. Examples of international target culture interactions were extremely rare although today English is used more and more among L2 speakers of English. In terms of cultural content, the textbooks dealt primarily with surface level aspects of culture such as food, names, customs, and school life.

Several of the dialogues in her data contained implicit assumptions as to the relationship between Japanese and western culture. The following dialogue, for example, subtly suggests that western culture should be emulated.

Rye: Jim?
Jim: What.
Rye: Is your father always doing the dishes like that?
Jim: Yes. My parents take turns cooking and doing the dishes.
Rye: My father never helps with the housework.
        He's too tired after a long day's work.
Jim: I think the Japanese work too much and too long.
        What do you think?
Rye: I think so too. But people are taking more holidays than before.
        My father stays home longer.
Jim: What does he do on holidays?
Rye: Usually, he just relaxes. But you know what?

He started to learn cooking.

Jim: Does he cook well?

Rye: Yes, he cooks very well.
       Everything is very very well-done.

(Source: *Echo.* 1997. Tokyo: Sanyusya, Lesson 18, "Housework," as cited in Iwasaki, 2000)

In light of the assumptions made in this dialogue regarding gender roles and western culture, a researcher could examine to what extent other dialogues in the text support or challenge these assumptions. To the extent that students focus more on what is said in an L2 text than how it is said, we need more research on the assumptions that exist in textbooks regarding ethnic identity, social class, and gender. Such research exemplifies a critical approach to L2 teaching and learning that seeks to challenge and change the existing social and political structure.

SUMMARY

In this chapter we examined various methods for studying classroom discourse. In terms of oral discourse we looked at two methods: interaction analysis and discourses analysis. Interaction analysis, by providing a coding scheme for analyzing classroom interaction, makes it possible to compare classroom discourse patterns across contexts. However, the complexity of such coding schemes often makes them difficult to use. In addition, the coding scheme limits what is salient to the researcher. Discourse analysis looks at a classroom interaction in the context of a particular teacher and learner in a specific classroom. The advantage of discourse analysis is that attention can be given to patterns as they arise from the data. The disadvantage is that the findings are limited to one particular context.

In discussing the analysis of written discourse using text analysis, we emphasized that the focus of text analysis can differ greatly. Whereas some text analysis involves an examination of the syntactic features of a text, other involves an examination of the rhetorical and cultural features of a text. In addition, although some text analysis involves counting discrete features of a text using predetermined categories such as T-units, other research examines the research data to develop unique categories for data analysis, such as categories regarding teachers' written feedback. Finally, some text analysis involves the use of corpora to evaluate and develop classroom materials. We ended the chapter by pointing out the possibility of adopting a critical approach to classroom materials research.

FURTHER READING

On Interaction Analysis

Chaudron, C. (1988). *Second language classrooms: Research on teaching and learning.* Cambridge, UK: Cambridge University Press.
Fanselow, J. (1987). *Breaking rules.* New York: Longman.
Spada, N., & Fröhlich, M. (1995). *COLT Observation Scheme.* Sydney: NCELTR, Macquarie University.

On Discourse Analysis

Have, P. (1999). *Doing conversation analysis.* London: Sage.
Lazaraton, A. (2002). Quantitative and qualitative approaches to discourse analysis. *Annual Review of Applied Linguistics, 22,* 32–51.
Markee, N. (2000). *Conversation analysis.* Mahwah, NJ: Lawrence Erlbaum Associates.
McCarthy, M. (1991). *Discourse analysis for language teachers.* Cambridge, UK: Cambridge University Press.

On Text Analysis

Grabe, W., & Kaplan, R. B. (1996). *Theory and practice of writing.* London: Addison Wesley Longman. (Chapter 2)

On Contrastive Rhetoric

Connor, U. (1996). *Contrastive rhetoric.* Cambridge, UK: Cambridge University Press.
Connor, U., & Kaplan, R. B. (Eds.). (1987). *Writing across languages. Analysis of L2 text.* Reading, MA: Addison Wesley.
Panetta, C. (Ed.). (2001). *Contrastive rhetoric revisited and redefined.* Mahwah, NJ: Lawrence Erlbaum Associates.

On Corpus-Based Research

Biber, D., & Conrad, S. (2001). Quantitative corpus-based research: Much more than bean counting. *TESOL Quarterly, 35*(2), 331–336.
Conrad, S. (1999). The importance of corpus-based research for language teachers. *System, 27,* 1–18.
Hunston, S. (2002). *Corpora in applied linguistics.* Cambridge, UK: Cambridge University Press.
McCarthy, M., & Carter, R. (2001). Size isn't everything: Spoken English, corpus and the classroom. *TESOL Quarterly, 35*(2), 337–340.

Chapter 4

Writing Research Reports

In this chapter we examine the following questions:

- What guidelines exist for writing theses and journal articles?
- What are the characteristics of effective research reports?

This chapter assumes that you have completed your research project, analyzed your data, and drawn your conclusions. Now you intend to summarize your research project as an academic paper, thesis, or publication. In this chapter we deal with issues that need to be addressed in any type of research report. We do, however, point out some of the ways in which the requirements of a thesis differ from a published article.

GUIDELINES

Thesis Guidelines

Our discussion of theses is directed to an American master's thesis as opposed to a doctoral thesis or dissertation. A master's thesis, of course, is more limited than a doctoral dissertation. Nevertheless, many of the features of effective research reports discussed in this chapter have relevancy for both a master's and doctoral thesis.

Most departments or universities have specific guidelines regarding the format of a thesis. In some instances the guidelines specify the organization of the thesis, typically adhering to a pattern similar to the following:

1. Introduction
2. Review of the literature
3. Methodology
4. Findings
5. Conclusions and implications

Although this pattern is useful for some types of theses, it may need to be modified for others, especially case studies and ethnographic studies. Some ethnographic studies, for example, begin with a discussion of the theoretical orientation of the study rather than a traditional review of the literature and some corpus-based studies contain no formal review of the literature.

The guidelines also often include a description of the requirements for the headings, paper quality, spacing, reference list, and binding. By carefully reviewing these guidelines before you begin to write, you avoid the need to do a good deal of reformatting later on. It is also a good idea to look at models of existing theses to get an idea of the organization and style of other theses at your university. Finally, be certain to consult the fair use guidelines regarding the extent to which copyrighted material can be cited so that you know what permissions you must obtain from publishers. We assume, of course, that by this point you have thoroughly reviewed the human subjects guidelines for your university and adhered fully to these guidelines.

*   *   *

Exploring the Ideas, 4.1

Consult the thesis guidelines for your university. Review the guidelines for

- *the organization of the thesis* (Do the guidelines have suggestions as to the major sections the thesis should contain? If so, what are they?),
- *the production of the thesis* (What are the requirements for the headings, paper quality, spacing, reference list, and binding?), and
- *the style guidelines* (Do the guidelines specify that a particular style must be used such as the American Psychological Association (APA) or Modern Language Association (MLA) format? If so, and you intend to write a thesis, obtain a copy of these guidelines).

Be prepared to share your findings with your classmates.

*   *   *

Exploring the Ideas, 4.2

Review a thesis completed at your own university that is of interest to you. Examine the following sections of the thesis and answer the questions listed below.

- Examine the *introduction* and problem statement. Is the problem that the study investigated clearly stated? Is there a clear statement of the rationale for the study?
- Examine the *literature review*. Has the author made it clear how the articles that are included in the review relate to the overall aims of the thesis? How is the literature review organized?
- Assess the *methods section* of the thesis. Have the participants and setting been described in detail? Are all the materials used in the study described in full and included in the thesis? Is the procedure that was followed described in sufficient detail that the study could be replicated?
- Study the *results section*. Has the author made it clear how the data were analyzed? Have the results been adequately summarized? Are tables used to summarize the findings and if so, are they referred to and explained in the text?
- Review the *conclusion*. Is there a summary of the purpose and findings of the study? Are the limitations of the study discussed? Does the conclusion contain pedagogical implications? Do these follow from the results of the study? Does the conclusion include any suggestions for further research?

Be prepared to share your findings with your classmates.

*　*　*

Journal Guidelines

There are several steps you should follow if you intend to submit a research report to a journal for publication.

1. Determine an Appropriate Journal

In order to determine what would be the most appropriate journal for the type of study you have undertaken, consider the kind of audience that would be most interested in your research. Because your research is classroom-based, you will likely want to submit your paper to an applied rather than theoretical journal. However, depending on the context of the study (EFL or ESL), the skills involved in the study, and the age of the students, there are journals more appropriate than others. The TESOL organization Web site includes a list of applied journals in the field of L2 teaching and learning, which is a useful place to find publication possibilities (http://www.tesol.edu/pubs/author/books/demystify.html).

Once you narrow down the choice to two or three journals, review what has been published in the journal during the past several years to determine the type of topics that appear to be of most interest to the readers of the journal. Also read a variety of articles included in the journal to get a sense of the organization and style that is typical of articles in the journal. Based on this review, decide which journal you believe would be most appropriate for your submission.

2. Review and Follow the Journal Guidelines

Once you decide on the most appropriate journal for your research, carefully review the guidelines for submission published in the journal. The amount of detail included in these guidelines varies from journal to journal, but typically it includes the topics that are of interest to the journal, the place to which articles should be submitted, the number of copies to submit, and the format of the paper. Typically there are also page limit guidelines; be certain to keep your paper within these guidelines, or this could be a basis for the editor to reject the manuscript. The journal may also have editors for specific sections of the journal so be certain to send the manuscript to the right editor. Most journals also assume that you have adhered to informed consent guidelines in gathering your data. Although they generally will not require you to submit the signed informed consent papers, they assume that you have these available. Some journals also specify particular guidelines for conducting and reporting both quantitative and qualitative studies.

3. Submit Your Manuscript

When you complete your manuscript, submit the correct number of copies to the editor with a cover letter that includes your full mailing and email address, along with a statement indicating that the manuscript is not being considered by any other journal. In general you should expect to hear within 3 to 4 weeks that your manuscript has been received and be given some idea as to how long the review process should take.

It is essential that you submit your manuscript to only one journal at a time. Most journals request that when you submit your manuscript, you indicate that the manuscript is not being considered by any other journal. This is done because reviewing a manuscript is a time-consuming process for editors and reviewers. Hence, the journal wants some guarantee that you are seriously submitting the manuscript to their journal and will let them make a decision regarding its appropriateness before you submit it to another journal.

4. Revise and Resubmit Your Manuscript

When you receive the reviews for your manuscript, study them carefully and remember that constructive criticism can result in even stronger reports. Don't be discouraged if your paper has not been accepted; almost all researchers have experienced rejections in submitting manuscripts. Additionally, very few manuscripts are immediately accepted for publication.

If your paper has not accepted for publication, you have several alternatives. If the paper has been rejected with no possibility for resubmission, you might consider revising the paper and sending it to another journal. In some cases, it is a matter of finding the right forum for a particular type of research investigation. If the reviewers suggest that you revise the paper and resubmit it to the same journal, consider the comments made by the reviewers with great care. Although many of the suggestions may be quite helpful in revising the paper, if you feel some of the suggestions do not contribute to the overall purpose of the paper, let the editor know which suggestions you have not followed and why. Your rationale for not following some of the suggestions could be included in an extended cover letter, accompanied by your revised manuscript.

*   *   *

Exploring the Ideas, 4.3

Review the guidelines for a journal to which you would someday like to submit a manuscript. Then answer the following questions. In some cases, the published guidelines will not provide the information on these topics, but you can get answers to these questions from the editor of the journal.

1. What topics are of interest to the journal?
2. What is the desired length of manuscript submissions?
3. How many copies should be submitted?
4. What style guidelines should be followed?
5. What kinds of articles does the journal accept (e.g., book reviews, commentaries, brief reports)
6. What ethical standards must be adhered to in the research?
7. What statistical guidelines and qualitative guidelines should be followed?

Be prepared to share your findings with your classmates.

* * *

RESEARCH REPORTS

Introductory Materials

Introduction

For both a thesis and journal publication, the introduction is a critical component of the paper. Not only must the introduction get the interest of the reader, but it should also explain how the research project has addressed an important gap in the field. Swales (1990) presents the following helpful model for introductions.

The first move in Swales' model is *establishing a territory* or introducing the topic of the research. The purpose of this move is to tell the audience how your study addresses an area of L2 teaching and learning that has wide interest and is related to previous research studies. For example, if your study deals with some aspect of the use of group work in an L2 classroom, you might refer to the growing interest in the use of group work associated

TABLE 4.1
Swales' Model for Research Report Introductions

Move 1 Establishing a territory
Step 1 Claiming centrality
and/or
Step 2 Making topic generalization(s)
and/or
Step 3 Reviewing items of previous research
Move 2 Establishing a niche
Step 1 Counter-claiming
and/or
Step 2 Indicating a gap
and/or
Step 3 Question-raising
and/or
Step 4 Continuing a tradition
Move 3 Occupying the niche
Step 1 Outlining the purpose of the research study
and/or
Step 2 Announcing the principal findings
and/or
Step 3 Indicating the structure of the research article

(Source: Adapted from Swales, 1990, p. 141)

with the increased popularity of communicative language teaching. Swales notes that there are several ways to establish a territory. You can

- describe the importance of the topic (i.e., *claiming centrality*; e.g., group work is a central component of many L2 classrooms today),
- show how the topic is applicable to a variety of contexts (i.e., *making topic generalizations*; e.g., group work can be used in ESL and EFL classrooms and in beginning and advanced classrooms), and/or
- briefly refer to some relevant research (i.e., *reviewing items of previous research*; e.g., refer to research on the use of group work that is relevant to your study).

The next move is *establishing a niche* in which you explain how your research is unique and significant. Here you can

- describe how your research challenges some existing research or beliefs (i.e., *counter-claiming*),
- show how your research addresses a topic that has not previously been examined (i.e., *indicating a gap*),
- introduce a question that you intend to answer in your report (i.e., *question-raising*), and/or
- explain how your research is part of an ongoing investigation in the field (i.e., *continuing a tradition*).

The final move, *occupying the niche*, involves describing what you will do in the paper. This section can include

- *outlining the purpose of the research study* (e.g., "This paper examines the use of the L1 in group work.")
- *announcing the principal findings* (e.g., "The use of the L1 serves a great variety of purposes in L2 group work.") and/or
- *indicating the structure of the research article* (e.g., "This paper reviews relevant literature on the use of group work and then describe the details of this study.").

Swales' model presents options for an introduction and clearly does not need to be followed exactly. Nonetheless, the model summarizes the major purposes of an introduction:

(a) to argue for the significance of the topic being discussed, and
(b) to explain how the study makes an important contribution to an understanding of L2 teaching and learning.

The following introduction from Kern's (1994) article on the role of mental translation in reading illustrates how some of these purposes can be addressed in an introductory paragraph.

> In the past 15 years, an impressive research effort has been directed toward understanding the processes involved in second language (L2) reading comprehension. Much of this research has consisted in the application of theoretical constructs developed in first language (L1) comprehension research (e.g., schemata, scripts, story grammars) to L2 reading situations. While this approach has been very productive, particularly in showing the importance of a reader's background knowledge in understanding L2 texts, it has not fully addressed one of the fundamental, self-evident differences between L1 and L2 comprehension: that the L2 reader has *two* languages at his or her disposal rather than just one. (p. 441)

Notice how in the paragraph Kern establishes a territory by *claiming the centrality* of the topic (i.e., "In the past 15 years, an impressive research effort has been directed to understanding the processes involved in second language (L2) reading comprehension"). He then *establishes a niche* by indicating a gap in the field, namely that previous research has not fully recognized the fact that an L2 reader has both his first and second language at his disposal. In the remainder of the introduction he *states the purpose of his research* (i.e., "to consider the multifaceted role that mental translation plays in L2 reading," p. 442) and briefly *outlines the structure of the article.*

In a thesis, the introduction is often a separate chapter in which the writer states the problem or problems that will be investigated and lists the questions or hypotheses that will be studied. The introduction also often provides a rationale for the study and discusses the theoretical orientation of the study. This introductory chapter is sometimes entitled the Introduction and Problem Statement.

*   *   *

Exploring the Ideas, 4.4

Analyze the introductions for two research articles that you have recently read. They can be articles you analyzed for other chapters in the book or articles you have read for a research study you are undertaking. For each article, answer the following questions:

1. How does the author *establish a territory*? Which steps listed under establishing a territory are included? Are steps other than those suggested by Swales included?

2. How does the author *establish a niche*? Does the author make a convincing argument for the significance of the study?

3. How does the author *occupy the niche*? Which steps listed under occupying the niche are included? Are steps other than those suggested by Swales included?

4. In your opinion is the introduction effective? Why or why not?

Be prepared to share your findings with your classmates.

* * *

Abstract

Because an abstract is often what readers use to decide whether or not to read a research report, it is a very important part of the report. Often there is a word limit that makes it necessary to very succinctly summarize the study. For both journal articles and theses, the abstract should contain a statement of the *purpose of the study, the methods used,* and *the findings.* The following abstract from the previously mentioned study by Kern (1994) illustrates how this information can be incorporated in a succinct abstract.

Reading in a second language (L2) can produce inefficient processing in otherwise proficient readers. This paper argues that mental translation during L2 reading may facilitate the generation and conservation of meaning by allowing the reader to represent portions of L2 texts that exceed cognitive limits in a familiar, memory-efficient form. Fifty-one intermediate-level French students, in high, middle, and low reading ability groups, participated in think-aloud interviews while reading French texts. The relative frequency of translation use among these groups is compared at the beginning and end of a semester and is found to decrease with level of reading ability. The specific contexts in which students relied on translation are identified, and functional benefits and strategic uses of translation are discussed. Finally, hypotheses and questions are developed for future research. (p. 441)

Notice now Kern begins with a general statement about L2 reading and then states the central argument of the paper. He then describes the content of the study, its methodology, and the kinds of findings that are reported.

The need to include a statement of purpose, method, and findings in an abstract is also needed for all types of qualitative studies. The following abstract from a discourse analysis study by Lazaraton (2003) on nonnative-English-speaking teachers illustrates these same moves.

This article examines incidental cultural knowledge displays by two nonnative-English-speaking teachers (NNESTs) in their intensive English program classrooms. Surprisingly, until recently, NNESTs have received little empirical attention in the literature, even though questions continue to arise about their language competence, pedagogical knowledge, and cultural orientation. This study goes beyond existing work on the impressions, reflections, and beliefs of NNESTs to ask, What is the nature of the discourse produced in ESL classes taught by NNESTs? And, more to the point, does an analysis of this discourse suggest real problems with language, teaching, or culture? An analysis of videotaped classroom data of two teachers indicated that a wide unpredictable range of cultural topics arose. Although with one exception they were able to deal with the cultural topics by displaying knowledge in a competent manner, the analysis suggested missed opportunities in that the teachers did not admit "I don't know," thus providing the chance for their students to become cultural informants in the classroom. (p. 213)

Notice how the abstract points out the gap that presently exists in the literature regarding the discourse of NNESTs in the classroom and describes the significance of the present study. These are important moves to include in both the abstract and the introduction.

* * *

Exploring the Ideas, 4.5

Analyze the abstracts for the two research articles your analyzed in *Exploring the Ideas, 4.4.* For each article, answer the following questions. In some cases the information may not be included.

1. What is the *purpose of the study*?
2. What *methods* are used in the study?
3. What are *the general findings* of the study?
4. Do you consider the abstract to be effectively written? Why or why not?

Be prepared to share your findings with your classmates.

* * *

Title

Another essential component of the introductory materials is the title. The title needs to summarize in a concise and creative manner the major purpose of the study. Because the title should generally be no more than 10 words long, it is necessary to select each word carefully. In order to provide readers with as much information as possible about the article, try to include words that succinctly state the *topic of the study* and *its context*, as is done in the title for the Lazaraton (2003) article previously discussed: "Incidental displays of cultural knowledge in the nonnative-English-speaking teacher's classroom."

In writing your title, you may want to use a colon to expand on the information included in the main heading (e.g., "Mediating language learning: Teacher interaction with ESL students in a content-based classroom," Gibbons, 2003) or to clarify the meaning of an interest-getting opener (e.g., "Simplicity without elegance: Features of L1 and L2 academic texts," Hinkel, 2003). Because the title is a reader's first introduction to a paper, it is useful to consider several titles and get feedback from colleagues on the titles.

* * *

Exploring the Ideas, 4.6

Review the titles listed in the Table of Contents for the last four issues of a journal you are interested in submitting a paper to someday. If you don't have access to the hard copy of the journal, many journals have a Table of Contents for the journal on the Web. Select several titles that you consider to be effective and several titles you believe are ineffective. Be prepared to provide reasons for why you think they are effective or ineffective.

* * *

Style

The introduction is also important in establishing a tone for your report. Although a thesis is generally descriptive with less room to express an author's voice, a journal article often clearly establishes the voice of the author. Notice in the following introductory paragraph how Edge (1996) takes a very humble stance as he looks at how the theoretical, professional, and personal lives of teachers interact. This stance is evident in the first paragraph of the paper where he states that his paper is personal, subjective, and based on inadequate knowledge.

This paper is personal. One connotation of personal is subjective; a related connotation is that one knows too little about the topic to make a valid generalization. Both connotations apply to this attempt to contribute to the study of what it means to be a person-who-teaches in the area of TESOL at the end of the 20th century. Generalisations, however, have not always served us well either in terms of how languages are learned or how they are taught, for they have all too often lost sight of the people concerned in the learning and teaching. Moreover it is at the level of the personal that theory-in-use (Argyris & Schon, 1974) is articulated in action. The fundamental theme of this paper is that the theoretical, the professional, and the personal intermingle. (p. 9)

On the other hand, Peirce (1995b) forcefully states her beliefs and assumptions in the opening to her article on the methodology of qualitative research. Notice how she uses the first person personal pronoun and verbs in the simple tense, "I examine" and "I take the position" to establish a tone of authority.

In this article I examine the complex relationship between theory and methodology in qualitative research. I take the position that theory (implicitly or explicitly) informs the questions researchers ask; the assumptions we make; and the procedures, methods, and approaches we use to carry out research projects. In turn, the questions asked will inevitably influence what kind of data are collected, how they are collected, and what conclusions are drawn on the basis of data analyses. (p. 569)

In deciding on the tone you wish to take, it is useful to consider your audience. Do you believe your audience shares your interests and assumptions? If not, you need to convince your audience that the topic you are investigating is significant and that the theoretical assumptions you are making are warranted.

* * *

Exploring the Ideas, 4.7

Examine the style and tone of the introductions you examined in *Exploring the Ideas, 4.4*. Try to characterize the tone that the author conveys. Is it humble as in the Edge article? Is it forceful and direct as in the Peirce article? What specific features of the text contribute to these qualities? Be prepared to share your analysis with classmates.

* * *

Literature Review

Organization

The introduction is typically followed by a literature review. A literature review can be a separate section or chapter occurring at the opening of a thesis or journal paper; it can also be integrated throughout the paper as support for particular topics addressed in the paper. The most common organization is to have the literature review as a separate section. However, with some action research studies, relevant literature is included in describing the research cycles. Additionally, in some ethnographic studies, the opening section establishes the theoretical framework for the study and relevant literature is cited within the paper.

The literature review is generally not a chronological account of previous studies. Rather the organization of what is summarized reflects the point you want to make regarding previous studies. For example, it may be that the purpose of your literature review is to demonstrate that the topic you are investigating is controversial. Imagine, for example, that you examined existing research on teacher feedback on student essays and you found that researchers have very different conclusions as to the benefits of teacher feedback. You could then cite studies that indicate feedback does contribute to the development of writing skills followed by a summary of those that indicate otherwise. In the article mentioned earlier by Lazaraton (2003), the author chose to organize the literature review according to various aspects of culture in language teaching: culture as curricular content, culture as social practice, and research on culture in language teaching and learning.

Swales and Feak (2000) suggest that in organizing the literature review you begin by developing some of type of matrix that categorizes the studies you read. For example, you might organize all of the articles you read by year of publication. This allows you to see if there has been any shift in widely held assumptions about a particular topic. You might also organize the studies by whether or not they occurred in ESL or EFL contexts or by whether they were done with high school or university students. As Swales and Feak (2000) point out, sorting what you read according to various criteria is beneficial in several ways: It allows a writer to get a general overview of the literature; it encourages a writer to make connections; and it permits the writer to make generalizations regarding what has previously been studied.

Purpose

For both a thesis and journal article, a literature review is a selective account of previous work on a topic that in some way is relevant to the present study. Although part of the purpose of a thesis literature review is to demonstrate that you have thoroughly reviewed the existing literature on the topic, it still should not be a mere recounting of everything you read. Remember the purpose of a literature review is to demonstrate how your study relates to previous studies. For example, in Chen and Graves (1995) referred to in chapter 1, Chen and Graves were interested in the effect of background knowledge and previewing in increasing reading comprehension. In the first part of their literature review they summarize existing studies on background knowledge. After doing so, they emphasize how the literature has shown the importance of background knowledge for reading. This fact provides support for their attention to background knowledge in their study. The following paragraph illustrates how they accomplish this.

> The findings of the above studies affirm that background knowledge plays an important role in learning and remembering text information. These findings provide convincing evidence for generalizing—as Person, Hansen, and Gordon (1979) did—that students with well-developed background knowledge comprehend text better than those with weakly developed background knowledge. This schema-theoretic generalization holds for all populations—young and old, native and non-native—and is especially significant for reading materials containing culture-specific elements which cannot be accessed without prior cultural knowledge. (Chen & Graves, 1995, p. 665)

In some instances you may want to critically evaluate the studies you cited, particularly if you believe their method or conclusions are in some way flawed. For example, in the Lazaraton (2003) study previously cited on displays of cultural knowledge by nonnative-English-speaking teachers, Lazaraton uses the literature review to summarize various views of culture in language teaching. In the first part of her review she discusses how culture can be viewed as curricular content. However, she is critical of this view of culture, stating, "The view of culture as unproblematic curricular content reflects a rather traditional and outdated perspective" (p. 216). Instead she supports a more updated view of culture, namely, a postmodern view of culture, which approaches "culture as a socially constructed practice" (p. 216).

*   *   *

Exploring the Ideas, 4.8

Examine the literature review of the articles you examined in *Exploring the Ideas, 4.4* and answer the following questions.

1. What is the overall organization pattern of the literature review?
2. Are the articles that are reviewed related to the present study? If so, select specific examples that illustrate how the author relates the literature review to the present study, as was shown above in the Chen and Graves article.
3. Does the author provide a critical review of any of the articles in the literature review? If so, provide a specific example of where this is done, as was shown in the previously mentioned Lazaraton study.

Be prepared to share your analysis with your classmates.

*   *   *

Citation Options

There are two widely used options for citing the authors of the studies referred to in a literature review. One is to directly give the author's name in the summary, using what Swales and Feak (2000) call an *integral citation*. The second is to cite the author in parenthesis or in a footnote, using what Swales and Feak call a *nonintegral citation*. The following is an example of each of these types of citations.

Integral Citation

Patton (1990) delineates three main types of interviews.

Nonintegral

Three main types of interview patterns exist (Patton 1990).

Because integral citations give more prominence to the authors, you should use these when you wish to emphasize the researcher.

Many verbs can be used to report the findings of other research studies. Hyland (1999) notes that the most commonly used verbs in the field of applied linguistics are *suggest, argue, show, explain, find,* and *point out.* The choice of reporting verb, of course, shows different attitudes of the researcher. The use of *claim,* for example, suggests that the researcher does not necessarily agree with what the author of the article is saying. On the other hand, the use of *show* suggests that the researcher does agree with the author. Williams (2004) terms these two types of reporting verbs *factive* verbs and *nonfactive* verbs. The use of *factive verbs* suggests that what is being discussed is an accepted fact. These include verbs such as *know, point out, prove, realize,* and *inform. Non-factive* verbs, on the other hand, express the attitude of the writer toward what is reported. These are verbs like *believe, claim, argue, assume, doubt, insist,* and *deny.* Which of these kinds of verbs to use depends on the attitude of the authors toward what they are reporting.

Swales and Feak (1994) note that the verb tense used in reporting verbs often signals different functions as shown below.

Pattern I—reference to a single study—*past tense*
(e.g., Leki, 1995, delineated various coping strategies that L2 writers use.)

Pattern II—reference to areas of inquiry that have relevance to the current study, often used in the passive voice—*present perfect tense*
(e.g., Several studies have investigated the reading strategies of L2 learners.)

Pattern III—reference to the state of current knowledge—*present tense*
(e.g., The causes of low motivation are complex.)

These are helpful generalization to keep in mind, though there are clearly many exceptions to these patterns.

*   *   *

Exploring the Ideas, 4.9

Examine the reporting verbs used in the literature review in one of the articles you have previously studied. In your analysis, answer the following questions.

1. Are integral or nonintegral citations more commonly used in the literature review? Select two examples of nonintegral citations and explain why you believe the author chose to give less prominence to the author in citing the work.
2. Underline the reporting verbs that are used. What verbs are most frequently used?
3. Notice the verb tenses used in the review of the literature. Find examples of the three patterns described by Swales and Feak (1994) previously shown.

Be prepared to share your analysis with your classmates.

*   *   *

Methodology

In both a thesis and journal article, the methodology should be reported in such detail that the study can be replicated. Frequently the methods section includes the following subtitles: *participants or subjects, materials, procedures,* and *analysis.* In order to illustrate how the methodology section can be organized in both quantitative and qualitative studies, the following discussion includes model paragraphs from each type of research.

Participants

In the participant section you should describe the characteristics of your participants, including such information as the subjects' age, gender, ethnicity, and linguistic background. You should also indicate on what basis you selected these particular participants. Finally, be certain to protect the anonymity of the participants by using pseudonyms or some other method of identification.

This information is illustrated in the following paragraph from the Chen and Graves (1995) quantitative study mentioned earlier on the effect of giving students previewing and background knowledge for a reading passage.

> Participants in the study were 243 students selected from more than 400 freshmen non-English majors attending Tamkang University, a 26,000-student private university in a Taipei suburb. According to school officials, the English proficiency of Tamkang freshmen is typically equivalent to that indicated by scores of 400 to 500 on the TOEFL. The 400 students were volunteers from two of Chen's and several of her colleagues' Freshman English classes. These students were chosen because Taiwanese college students are required to take Freshman English and part of the course attempts to introduce them to English and American literature through their reading of short stories, plays and poems. (p. 667)

The qualitative study by Lazaraton (2003) on NNESTs, mentioned earlier, includes the following paragraph on the subjects of the study.

> The data for this article come from a larger study of two MA ESL graduate students who were employed as teaching assistants (TAs) in an intensive English program (IEP) affiliated with an MA ESL program in a large university in the U.S. Midwest. The data were collected during the spring semester 2001 and consist of six 50-minute videotaped classes (three for each teacher), or approximately 300 minutes of classroom interaction. The two teachers (referred to here as TE1 and TE2) were chosen because they were the only nonnative-English-speaking MA ESL students employed in the IEP at the time of data collection. . . . (p. 220)

Notice how Lazaraton provides a rationale for the selection of the participants. Later, she gives further details on the characteristics of the two teachers as well as the students who participated in the videotaped classes.

Materials

The materials section should include a description or copy of any research instruments you used. For example, if you used a survey or interview to gather data, this instrument should be included in the report, most likely in an appendix. If you used a reading passage as the basis for a verbal protocol, this too should appear in the report. If you employed a particular coding system in observing an L2 classroom, you should include a copy of this coding system; if you modified an existing coding system, you should indicate what changes you made in the existing coding system.

The following opening paragraph to the materials section from the Chen and Graves (1995) study summarizes what materials the authors used in their study. Additionally, the study includes the preview and background knowledge passages for the short story in an appendix to the article.

> Materials included one American short story and one American autobiographical narrative. For each selection, there were a preview, an expository passage of background information, a passage containing both a preview and background knowledge, a pretest, and a posttest composed of 15 short-answer questions and 15 multiple-choice items. Materials also included directions for administering the treatments, a teacher information form, a study consent form, a personal data form, a participant debriefing form, a semantic differential, and an open-ended question. All materials were written and presented in English. (p. 668)

In Lazaraton (2003) no separate section on materials is included since no materials other than the videotaped classes were used in the study.

Procedures

The procedure section is generally the most detailed of the methods section. In this section, you need to describe exactly what you did in undertaking the study. For example, if your study involved think-alouds, you need to describe in detail how you prepared the participants for the think-aloud, what role you played while the students were engaged in the think-aloud, and whether or not you engaged in a reflective interview with the participants when the think-aloud was finished. If you conducted a survey, you should indicate whether or not you piloted the survey instrument and with whom and how you administered the survey. If you analyzed the written comments on student essays, you should describe how you acquired the group of essays you analyzed and how you analyzed them. In the procedure section, you should also describe any modifications you needed to make to your original research plan. For example, perhaps you wanted to have six focal students in your case study but two dropped out for personal reasons. Or it may be that you wanted to observe a certain number or type of L2 classes but for practical reasons this was not possible.

The following opening paragraphs from the procedure section of the Chen and Graves (1995) study summarizes what information is included in the procedures section of the study.

> Students were classified as either high achieving or low achieving based on a median split on their total English scores on the required Joint College Entrance Examination (Ministry of Education, Taiwan, 1992), which they took before entering the university. Equal numbers of high achieving and low achieving students were then randomly assigned to one of the experimental groups or the control group.
>
> The pretests, treatments, and immediate posttests spanned 3 weeks. The pretests were given in the first week, the first story and its posttests in the sec-

ond week, and the second story, its posttests, and the attitude survey in the third week. In the following sections, the pretest, treatment, and survey procedures are discussed in detail. (p. 670)

In the Lazaraton (2003) study the procedures section is entitled Data Collection. In this section, Lazaraton describes how she approached the two teachers for permission to videotape their classes. Once she obtained permission from them to tape three of their classes, she talked to the students and obtained written consent from the two teachers and all of the students. The following paragraphs describe Lazaraton's procedures.

> The two teachers were approached for permission to videotape a negotiable number of classes. They were informed about the general purpose of the research (to look at ESL classroom discourse) but not the specific questions that might be asked. Both teachers decided that a maximum of three classes during the 14-week semester could be videotaped without the process being overly intrusive. As a result, they agreed to be videotaped once a month for 3 months. The recording room was reserved well in advance of the taping dates; the teachers were free to teach whatever they chose during those classes.
>
> Once they had granted their permission, the teachers talked to their students, who also consented to be videotaped. I obtained the informed, written consent of the two teachers and all 41 students before any videotaping took place. University Language Center personnel in a neighboring room behind a one-way mirror videotaped the classes in a classroom equipped with several external microphones suspended from the ceiling, one Sound Grabber table microphone in the front of the room and two mounted remote-controlled upper-corner cameras. (p. 221)

Analysis

Finally, in the analysis section you should describe how you went about analyzing the data. With some qualitative data, such as interview data, most researchers review the data several times looking for patterns. In chapter two we described how Borg (1998) followed this procedure with his interview data. If you used a coding system for a classroom observation or think-aloud, you may have reviewed several existing coding schemes and combined some of these to suit your purposes. If you modified an existing scheme you should describe in what way you modified it. You also want to clarify whether or not you had a second rater check your coding and if so, you should describe the background of this individual and the degree of inter-rater reliability. If you checked your own coding, you should indicate your intra-rater reliability.

Chen and Graves (1995) in their analysis section describe the statistical procedures they used to assess which pre-reading procedure resulted in the best comprehension of the reading selections. In the analysis section of the

Lazaraton (2003) article, entitled Data Transcript and Analysis, Lazaraton describes how the audiotapes were transcribed and inductively analyzed. She describes the analysis of the data in the following manner.

> Consistent with CA [conversational analysis] prescriptions, then, the video-taped data collected for the study were segmented into turns of talk, which were carefully transcribed, using CA notation. Additionally, the research questions posed in this research were not formulated prior to analyzing data; rather, they emerged from the data and were formulated, in part, so that the article would conform to standard guidelines for research reporting. . . . (p. 223)

She points out that no coding or counts of the data occurred because her purpose was to understand single cases and not aggregates of data.

*   *   *

Exploring the Ideas, 4.10

Examine the methodology section of one of the articles you have previously studied. In your analysis, answer the following questions.

1. Who were the *participants* involved in the study? Is there any additional information you would like to have on these participants?
2. What *materials* were used in the study? Are copies of any of these materials included in the article? Do you think any other materials used in the study should have appeared in the article?
3. What *procedures* were followed in the study? Would you like to have any further information on the procedures?
4. How were the data analyzed? Would you like to have any additional information on the data analysis?

Be prepared to share your analysis with your classmates.

*   *   *

Findings and Discussion

Organization

There are various ways to organize the findings of your study. If you undertook a case study of several students, you might choose to organize your results section by summarizing each student in the case study, or if you developed categories from your data analysis you can use these categories as the basis for your organization. Leki (1995), for example, organized part of her results section according to the coping strategies the students in her study used to meet the demands of their academic writing, such as looking for models, relying on past writing experiences, and resisting teachers' demands. In her study of the discourse of NNEST teachers, Lazaraton (2003) chose to organize her findings according to cultural topics that were addressed in the ESL classes she videotaped. These included copyright issues, Minnesota weather, swearing, the governor, and drug trafficking.

Perhaps the most challenging type of research findings to organize is the data gathered in ethnographic studies. Because of the complexity and richness of the data gathered, the researcher is left with a good deal of information to organize in some coherent fashion. By reviewing the data over and over again, the researcher typically discovers patterns that can form the basis for organizing the results section. Harklau (1994), for example, in her ethnographic study of 4 Chinese immigrant students' experience in their ESL and mainstream classes, describes her results according to the organization of instruction and language use in both ESL classes and mainstream classes. Her subcategories include spoken language used in mainstream classes and in ESL classes, written language used in both contexts, explicit language instruction, and the socializing function of schooling.

Tables

For many kinds of studies, using tables to summarize the findings is an effective strategy. If the study is survey research, tables can be used to summarize the answers given on the survey. If the study analyzed some type of discourse such as verbal protocols or teacher student conferences, tables can be used to summarize the number of occurrences of particular categories of the coding system. For example, Goldstein and Conrad (1990) in their results section include a table that shows the episodes per conference for each student they studied in terms of (a) the conversational work done primarily by the teacher; (b) the student/teacher sharing work; and (c) the conversational work done primarily by the student.

The *Publication Manual of the American Psychological Association* (1994) has a variety of suggestions for the use of tables. To begin, it suggests that because tables are difficult to set and may be complicated to read, they should be reserved only for crucial data that is directly related to the content of the study. They also include the following advice about the use of tables.

- The information included in a table should supplement and not duplicate what is in the text.
- Every table included in the article should be referred to in the text and its meaning clarified for the reader.

- Each table should be intelligible in its own right so that it can be understood without referring to the text.
- Tables should be referred to by the table number in the text and not by the page number of the article.
- All tables should be numbered with Arabic numbers in the order they appear in the text.
- All tables should have a brief and explanatory title.
- Each column in a table should also have a heading that is short and clear.

* * *

Exploring the Ideas, 4.11

Review the tables included in a research article you have read and answer the following questions.

1. Is the information included in the table clear?
2. Is the table referred to in the text and its significance explained?
3. Are the tables referred to in the text by their numbers?
4. Are the headings of the tables short and explanatory?
5. Are all of the columns in the table labeled?

Be prepared to share your findings with your classmates.

* * *

Examples from the Data

In some types of studies, examples from the data are included to illustrate some of the issues that are discussed. These examples can include quotes from interviews, excerpts of classroom interaction, or excerpts from diaries and journals. Lazaraton (2003) includes excerpts from the classes she observed that illustrate the cultural topics that were dealt with in the class. Peirce (1995a) in her case study of Canadian immigrant women's struggle to use English includes excerpts from the women's diaries to illustrate the kinds of struggles these women faced in using English and what caused them to overcome these obstacles. For example, in the following excerpt, one of the women describes her experience in using the phone in English.

5. The first time I was very nervous and afraid to talk on the phone. When the phone rang, everybody in my family was busy, and my daughter had to answer it. After ESL course when we moved and our

landlords tried to persuade me that we have to pay for the whole year, I got upset and I talked with him on the phone over one hour and I didn't think about the tenses rules. I had known that I couldn't give up. My children were very surprised when they heard me. (p. 22)

As is clear from the example above, well-chosen excerpts are very convincing data. In selecting the excerpts to include, select ones that illustrate the point you wish to make and clarify how the example demonstrates the issue at hand. In addition use excerpts that fairly represent the data gathered. Each example should be numbered consecutively throughout the paper. Also if the examples in the paper come from more than once source, label the source of the data (e.g., interviews, journals, diaries) and the date gathered. As was mentioned in chapter l, the dependability of qualitative research depends on being able to document the source of the evidence used.

*   *   *

Exploring the Ideas, 4.12

Reread a qualitative research article you are familiar with that includes examples from the data. Evaluate the examples according to the following criteria.

1. Do the examples effectively illustrate the point that the author is making? Has the researcher made it clear how the example relates to the issue at hand?
2. Is the source of the data clearly specified?
3. Are the examples numbered throughout the paper?

Be prepared to share your assessment with your classmates.

*   *   *

Conclusion

Depending on your audience, you may want to include a separate section on the pedagogical implications of your study in your conclusion. If the journal is an applied journal, this, of course, is of great interest to the audience. On the other hand, you could also mention the pedagogical implications of your study in the conclusion. Harklau (1994), for example, in her conclusion made specific suggestions regarding the way in which both mainstream and ESL language education could become more responsive to the needs of newly arrived immigrant students.

The conclusion itself can have a variety of moves, among them the following:

- A summary of the major findings of the study
- A call for further research on questions raised by the study
- A statement of the limitations of the study
- A repetition of a theme or issue raised in the introduction
- An explanation of the pedagogical implications of the study
- A statement of the overall significance of the topic addressed in the study.

No matter which of these moves is included, the conclusion should end on a strong note with some general statement that leaves the reader with a positive sense of the article.

The conclusion of the Kern (1994) study on mental translation in reading, mentioned earlier in the chapter, illustrates several of these moves. As part of the conclusion Kern lists hypothesis that can be drawn from his study.

> The findings of this study lead to two principle hypotheses related to translation during reading:
> 1. Mental translation during L2 reading can facilitate the generation and conservation of meaning by allowing the reader to represent portions of L2 text that exceed cognitive limits in a familiar, memory-efficient form.
> 2. As L2 learners become more proficient at reading L2 texts, they will rely less on translation in their efforts to comprehend. (p. 455)

Kern then discusses many research questions that are related to these hypotheses such as whether or not certain types of texts encourage more frequent use of translation than others and what explains the eventual decrease in translation use. This is followed by an entire paragraph on the pedagogical implications of his study for L2 instruction and testing. For example, he points out that because translation can foster reading comprehension, it should not be discouraged. In his final paragraph, he refers back to the idea made in his introduction on the importance of recognizing that bilingual readers have at their disposal two languages, and he urges more research on the role of L1 in L2 reading. He states,

> Understanding the role the native language plays in L2 reading comprehension is an important objective in the development of L2 reading. It is hoped that further research exploring the manifold ways in which L1 influences L2 reading comprehension processes will expand and shed light on the questions raised in this study. (p. 456)

Lazaraton (2003) chose to organize her conclusion into two sections. One entitled Limitations, Implications, and Future Research and the second Conclusion. In her conclusion, she restates the primary purpose of the article and makes a general call for more research on the topic.

> My primary purpose in this article has been to suggest that a systematic discourse analysis of classroom data provides unique insights into the complex relationships that exist among and between language, culture and teaching for NNESTs and the means by which their classroom culture is constructed. It is hoped that an empirical, classroom discourse-based research agenda on both the NEST and the NNEST emerges from this work and that other applied linguists continue to analyze, in a systematic and microanalytic fashion, not just the cultural knowledge required of and displayed by the ESL teacher but the many other important aspects of pedagogical performance in the L2 classroom. (p. 241)

Because the conclusion of a study plays an important function in demonstrating the value of the study, be sure to review your conclusion carefully so that it presents a clear summary of the article, along with a strong statement regarding the significance of the study.

*   *   *

Exploring the Ideas, 4.13

Reread two articles you are familiar with, answering the following questions on the conclusion of each article.

1. Does the conclusion include a summary of the research report?
2. Does the article refer back to any issues or themes raised in the opening of the paper?
3. If the conclusion includes a call for further research, what type of research is advocated?
4. If the conclusion includes a statement of the pedagogical implications of the study, what are they?
5. Does the conclusion highlight the significance of the study? If so. what does the author view at its significance?

Be prepared to share your review with your classmates.

*   *   *

SUMMARY

In this chapter, we examined the writing of research reports, specifically theses and journal articles. We began by pointing out the importance of consulting published guidelines for both a thesis and journal article before beginning to do any writing. Consulting these guidelines beforehand will insure that your paper meets the specified length and formatting requirements. We then considered the writing of introductions, emphasizing the need to use the introduction to get the readers' attention, state the purpose of the research project, and indicate how the research fills an existing gap in the literature. In discussing the literature review, we noted how the review should be selective and include only literature that is relevant to the overall purpose of the research project. In describing the methodology of a study, we pointed out that this section should include sufficient detail about the participants, materials, procedures, and data analyses so the study can be replicated. The manner in which the findings of the study are organized will differ with the type of research undertaken, with case studies and ethnographic research being much less predictable in their organization. The conclusion of the paper should summarize the results of the study, highlight its significance, and point out the pedagogical implications of the study.

FURTHER READING

On Dissertation Writing

Madsen, D. (1992). *Successful dissertations and theses.* San Francisco, CA: Jossey-Bass.
Mauch, J., & Birch, J. (1998) *Guide to the successful thesis and dissertation.* New York: Marcel Dekker.

On Research Reports

American Psychological Association. (1994) *Publication manual of the American psychological association* (4th ed.). Washington, DC.
Swales, J. (1990). *Genre analysis: English in academic and research settings.* Cambridge, UK: Cambridge University Press.
Swales, J., & Feak, C. (2000). *English in today's research world: A writing guide.* Ann Arbor: University of Michigan Press.

References

Allen, P., Fröhlich, M., & Spada, N. (1984). The communicative orientation of language teaching: An observation scheme. In J. Handscombe, R. Orem, & B. Taylor (Eds.), *On TESOL '83: The question of control* (pp. 231–252). Washington, DC: TESOL.

Allwright, D., & Bailey, K. M. (1991). *Focus on the language classroom.* Cambridge, UK: Cambridge University Press.

Atkinson, J. M., & Heritage, J. (Eds.). (1984). *Structure of social action: Studies in conversation analysis.* Cambridge, UK: Cambridge University Press.

Auerbach, E. (1986). Competency-based ESL: One step forward or two steps back? *TESOL Quarterly, 20*(3), 411–430.

Bailey, K. M. (1983). Competitiveness and anxiety in adult second language learning: Looking at and through the diary studies. In H. W. Selinger & M. H. Long (Eds.), *Classroom oriented research in second language acquisition* (pp. 67–103). Rowley, MA: Newbury House.

Bailey, K. M. (1990). The use of diary studies in teacher education programs. In J. C. Richards & D. Nunan (Eds.), *Second language teacher education* (pp. 215–240). Cambridge, UK: Cambridge University Press.

Bailey, K. M. (1991). Diary studies of classroom language learning: The doubting game and the believing game. In E. Sadtono (Ed.), *Language acquisition and the second/foreign language classroom* (pp. 60–102). Singapore: SEAMEO Regional Language Center.

Bailey, K. M., & Ochsner, R. (1983). A methodological review of the diary studies: Windmill tilting or social science? In K. M. Bailey, M. H. Long, & S. Peck (Eds.), *Second language acquisition studies* (pp. 188–198). Rowley, MA: Newbury House.

Bardovi-Harlig, & Dornyei, Z. (1998). Do language learners recognize pragmatic violations? Pragmatic versus grammatical awareness in instructed L2 learning. *TESOL Quarterly, 32*(2), 233–262.

Bellello, M. (2003). *Why some ESL writers are better than others.* Unpublished manuscript.

Biber, D., & Conrad, S. (2001). Quantitative corpus-based research: Much more than bean counting. *TESOL Quarterly, 35*(2), 331–336.

Biber, D., Johansson, S., Leech, G., Conrad, S., & Finegan, E. (1999). *Longman grammar of spoken and written English.* London: Longman.

Block, D. (2000). Problematizing interview data: Voices in the mind's machine? *TESOL Quarterly, 34*(4), 757–768.

Block, E. (1986). The comprehension strategies of second language readers. *TESOL Quarterly, 20*(3), 463–494.

Bond, A. (1998). Dealing with different learning styles. In J. C. Richards (Ed.), *Teaching in action* (pp. 176–179). Alexandria, VA: TESOL.

Borg, S. (1998). Teachers' pedagogical systems and grammar teaching: A qualitative study. *TESOL Quarterly, 32*(1), 9–38.

Brown, J. D. (1988). *Understanding research in second language.* Cambridge, UK: Cambridge University Press.

Brown, J. D. (2001). *Using surveys in language programs.* Cambridge, UK: Cambridge University Press.

Brown, J. D., & Rodgers, T. S. (2002). *Doing second language research.* Oxford, UK: Oxford University Press.

Burns, A. (1999). *Collaborative action research for English teachers.* Cambridge, UK: Cambridge University Press.

Cameron, D., Frazer, E., Harvey, P., Rampton, M. B. H., & Richardson, K. (Eds.). (1992). *Researching language: Issues of power and method.* London, UK: Routledge.

Celce-Murcia, M., & Olshtain, E. (2000). *Discourse and context in language teaching.* Cambridge, UK: Cambridge University Press.

Chaudron, C. (1988). *Second language classrooms: Research on teaching and learning.* Cambridge, UK: Cambridge University Press.

Chen, H.-C., & Graves, M. F. (1995). Effects of previewing and providing background knowledge on Taiwanese college students' comprehension of American short stories. *TESOL Quarterly, 29*(4), 663–686.

Chick, J. K. (1996). Intercultural communication. In S. L. McKay & N. Hornberger (Eds.), *Sociolinguistics and language teaching* (pp. 329–348). Cambridge, UK: Cambridge University Press.

Cohen, L., Manion, L., & Morrison, K. (2000). *Research methods in education.* London, UK: Routledge Falmer.

Connor, U. (1994). Text Analysis. *TESOL Quarterly, 28*(4), 682–684.

Connor, U. (1996). *Contrastive rhetoric.* Cambridge, UK: Cambridge University Press.

Connor, U., & Kaplan, R. B. (Eds.). (1987). *Writing across languages: An analysis of L2 text.* Reading, MA: Addison Wesley.

Conrad, S. (1999). The importance of corpus-based research for language teachers. *System, 27,* 1–18.

Cortazzi, M., & Jin, L. (1999). Cultural mirrors: Materials and methods in the EFL classroom. In E. Hinkel (Ed.), *Culture in second language teaching and learning* (pp. 196–219). Cambridge, UK: Cambridge University Press.

Cowie, N. (2001). An "It's not action research yet, but I'm getting there" approach to teaching writing. In J. Edge (Ed.), *Action research* (pp. 21–33). Alexandria, VA: TESOL.

Coxhead, A. (2000). A new academic word list. *TESOL Quarterly, 34*(2), 213–238.

Dawkins, R. (2003). *A devil's chaplain: Reflections on hope, lies, science, and love.* Boston: Houghton Mifflin Company.

Dornyei, Z. (2003). *Questionnaires in second language research.* Mahwah, NJ: Lawrence Erlbaum Associates.

Duff, P. (1995). An ethnography of communication in immersion classrooms in Hungary. *TESOL Quarterly, 29*(3), 505–536.

Edge, J. (1996). Cross-cultural paradoxes in a profession of values. *TESOL Quarterly, 30*(1), 9–30.

Edge, J. (2001). *Action research.* Alexandria, VA: TESOL.

Ericsson, K. A., & Simon, H. A. (1993). *Protocol analysis.* Cambridge, MA: The MIT Press.

Fang, X., & Warschauer, M. (2004). Technology and curricular reform in China: A case study. *TESOL Quarterly, 38*(2), 301–324.

Fanselow, J. (1987). *Breaking rules.* New York: Longman.

Ferris, C. (1997). The influence of teacher commentary on student revision. *TESOL Quarterly, 31*(2), 315–339.

Ferris, D. (1994). Rhetorical strategies in student persuasive writing: Differences between native and non-native English speakers. *Research in the Teaching of English, 28*(1), 45–65.

Fetterman, D. (1989). *Ethnography step by step.* Newbury Park, CA: Sage.

Flowerdew, J., & Miller, L. (1995). On the notion of culture in second language lectures. *TESOL Quarterly, 29*(2), 345–374.

Flowerdew, L. (2003). A combined corpus and systemic-functional analysis of the problem-solution pattern in a student and professional corpus of technical writing. *TESOL Quarterly, 37*(3), 489–512.

Frazier, S. (2003). A corpus analysis of *would*-clauses without adjacent if-clauses. *TESOL Quarterly, 37*(3), 443–466.

Freeman, D. (1998). *Doing teacher research.* New York: Heinle & Heinle.

Fukuda, Y. (2003a). *Error treatment in oral communication classes in Japanese high schools.* Unpublished Master's Thesis, San Francisco State University, San Francisco.

Fukuda, Y. (2003b). *Summary of my master's thesis: Treatment of spoken errors in Japanese high school oral communication classes.* Unpublished manuscript.

Gass, S., & Mackey, A. (2000). *Stimulated recall methodology in second language research.* Mahwah, NJ: Lawrence Erlbaum Assoiactes.

Gibbons, P. (2003). Mediating language learning: Teacher interactions with ESL students in a content-based classroom. *TESOL Quarterly, 37*(2), 247–274.

Gilmore, A. (2004). A comparison of textbook and authentic interactions. *ELT Journal, 58*(4), 363–374.

Goh, C. M. (2002). Exploring listening comprehension tactics and their interaction patterns. *System, 30,* 185–206.

Goldstein, L., & Conrad, S. (1990). Student input and negotiation of meaning in ESL writing conferences. *TESOL Quarterly, 24*(3), 443–460.

Grabe, W., & Kaplan, R. B. (1996). *Theory and practice of writing.* London, UK: Addison Wesley Longman.

Gu, Y. (2003). Fine brush and freehand: The vocabulary learning art of two successful Chinese EFL learners. *TESOL Quarterly, 37*(1), 73–104.

Hancock, M. (1997). Behind classroom code switching: Layering and language choice in L2 learner interaction. *TESOL Quarterly, 31*(2), 217–236.

Harklau, L. (1994). ESL versus mainstream classes: Contrasting L2 learning environments. *TESOL Quarterly, 28*(2), 241–272.

Have, P. (1999). *Doing conversation analysis.* London: Sage.

Hinkel, E. (1995). The use of modal verbs as a reflection of cultural values. *TESOL Quarterly, 29*(2), 325–344.

Hinkel, E. (2003). Simplicity without elegance: Features of sentences in L1 and L2 academic texts. *TESOL Quarterly, 37*(2), 275–302.

Hinkel, E. (2004). Tense, aspect and the passive voice in L1 and L2 academic texts. *Language Teaching Research, 8*(1), 5–29.

Homburg, T. J. (1984). Holistic evaluation of ESL compositions: Can it be validated objectively? *TESOL Quarterly, 18,* 87–107.

Hornberger, N. (1994). Ethnography. *TESOL Quarterly, 28*(4), 688–690.

Horowitz, D. (1986). Essay examination prompts and the teaching of academic writing. *English for Specific Purposes, 5*(2), 107–120.

Hunston, S. (2002). *Corpora in applied linguistics.* Cambridge, UK: Cambridge University Press.

Hunt, K. (1965). *Grammatical structures written at three grade levels.* Urbana, IL: National Council of teachers of English.

Hyland, K. (1999). Academic attribution: Citation and the construction of disciplinary knowledge. *Applied Linguistics, 20,* 341–367.

Hyland, K. (2002). *Teaching and researching writing.* London, UK: Longman.

Igarashi, M. (2003). *An analysis of writing conferences in college ESL composition.* Unpublished manuscript.

Ishikawa, S. (1995). Objective measurement of low-proficiency ESL narrative writing. *Journal of Second Language Writing, 4*(1), 51–70.

Iwasaki, S. (2000). *Evaluating cultural context and content in EFL materials: A study of high school level oral communication textbooks in Japan.* Paper presented at the TESOL Convention 2000, Vancouver, Canada.

Jenkins, S., & Hinds, J. (1987). Business letter writing: English, French, and Japanese. *TESOL Quarterly, 21*(2), 327–354.

Johnson, D. (1992). *Approaches to research in second language learning.* New York: Longman.

Jones, L. (2002). *Let's talk, Book 3.* Cambridge, UK: Cambridge University Press.

Kamhi-Stein, L. D. (2003). Reading in two languages: How attitudes toward home language and beliefs about reading affect the behaviors of "underprepared" L2 college readers. *TESOL Quarterly, 37*(1), 35–71.

Kaplan, R. B. (1966). Cultural thought patterns in intercultural education. *Language Learning, 16,* 1–20.

Kaplan, R. B. (2001). Foreword: What in the world is contrastive rhetoric? In C. G. Panetta (Ed.), *Contrastive rhetoric revisited and redefined* (pp. vii–xx). Mahwah, NJ: Lawrence Erlbaum Associates.

Kasper, G. (1998). Analysing verbal protocols. *TESOL Quarterly, 32*(2), 358–362.

Kemmis, S., & McTaggart, R. (Eds.). (1992). *The action research planner.* Geeloong, Victoria, Australia: Deakin University Press.

Kern, R. G. (1994). The role of mental translation in second language reading. *Studies in Second Language Acquisition, 16*(4), 441–461.

Kroll, B., & Reid, J. (1994). Guidelines for designing writing prompts: Clarifications, caveats, and cautions. *Journal of Second Language Writing, 3*(3), 231–255.

Kumaravadivelu, B. (1999). Critical classroom discourse analysis. *TESOL Quarterly, 33*(3), 453–484.

Labov, W. (1982). Objectivity and commitment in linguistic science: The case of the Black English trial in Ann Arbor. *Language in Society, 11,* 165–201.

Land, & Whitley, C. (1989). Evaluating second language essays in regular composition classes: Toward a pluralistic U.S. rhetoric. In D. Johnson & D. Roen (Eds.), *Richness in writing* (pp. 284–293). New York: Longman.

Lazaraton, A. (2002). Quantitative and qualitative approaches to discourse analysis. *Annual Review of Applied Linguistics, 22,* 32–51.

Lazaraton, A. (2003). Incidental displays of cultural knowledge in the nonnative-English-speaking teacher's classroom. *TESOL Quarterly, 37*(2), 213–246.

Leki, I. (1995). Coping strategies of ESL students in writing tasks across the curriculum. *TESOL Quarterly, 29*(2), 235–260.

Li, D. (1998). "It's always more difficult than you plan and imagine": Teachers' perceived difficulties in introducing the communicative approach in South Korea. *TESOL Quarterly, 32*(4), 677–703.

Lincoln, Y. S., & Guba, E. G. (1985). *Naturalistic inquiry.* Beverley Hills: Sage.

Liu, D. (2003). The most frequently used spoken American English idioms: A corpus analysis and its implications. *TESOL Quarterly, 37*(4), 671–700.

Madsen, D. (1992). *Successful dissertations and theses.* San Francisco, CA: Jossey-Bass.

Mangelsdorf, K. (1992). Peer review in the ESL composition classroom: What do the students think. *ELT Journal, 46*(3), 274–284.

Markee, N. (2000). *Conversation analysis.* Mahwah, NJ: Lawrence Erlbaum Associates.

Matsuda, A. (2002). Representation of users and uses of English in beginning Japanese EFL textbooks. *JALT Journal, 24*(2), 182–200.

Mauch, J., & Birch, J. (1998). *Guide to the successful thesis and dissertation.* New York: Marcel Dekker.

McCarthy, M. (1991). *Discourse analysis for language teachers.* Cambridge: Cambridge University Press.

McCarthy, M., & Carter, R. (2001). Size isn't everything: Spoken English, corpus and the classroom. *TESOL Quarterly, 35*(2), 337–340.

McDonough, J., & McDonough, S. (1997). *Research methods for English language teachers.* London: Arnold.

McKay, S. (Ed.). (1984). *Composing in a second language.* Rowley, MA: Newbury House.

Miles, M. B., & Huberman, A. M. (1994). *Qualitative data analysis.* London: Sage.

Minami, S. (in press). Sustained-content reading and its effect on reading comprehension. *Journal of Minami Kywshu Junior College.*

Mohan, B. A., & Lo, W. A. (1985). Academic writing and Chinese students: Transfer and developmental factors. *TESOL Quarterly, 19*(3), 515–534.

Nakahama, Y., Tyler, A., & van Lier, L. (2001). Negotiation of meaning in conversational and information gap activities: A comparative discourse analysis. *TESOL Quarterly, 35*(3), 377–405.

Newell, A., & Simon, H. A. (1972). *Human problem solving.* Englewood Cliffs, NJ: Prentice-Hall.

NIH. (2002). *Human participant protections education for research teams.* Unpublished manuscript.

Numrich, C. (1996). On becoming a language teacher: Insights from diary studies. *TESOL Quarterly, 30*(1), 131–154.

Nunan, D. (1992). *Research methods in language learning.* Cambridge, UK: Cambridge University Press.

O'Keeffe, A., & Farr, F. (2003). Using language corpora in initial teacher education: Pedagogic issues and practical applications. *TESOL Quarterly, 37*(3), 389–418.

O'Kelly, T. A. (1998). When students won't use English in class. In J. C. Richards (Ed.), *Teaching in action* (pp. 187–190). Alexandra, VA: TESOL.

Panetta, C. G. (Ed.). (2001). *Contrastive rhetoric revisited and redefined.* Mahwah, NJ: Lawrence Erlbaum Publishers.

Patton, M. Q. (1990). *Qualitative evaluation and research methods.* Newbury Park, CA: Sage.

Peirce, B. N. (1995a). Social identity, investment and language learning. *TESOL Quarterly, 29*(1), 9–31.

Peirce, B. N. (1995b). The theory of methodology in qualitative research. *TESOL Quarterly, 29*(3), 569–576.

Prodromou, L. (1992). What culture? Which culture? Cross-cultural factors in language learning. *ELT Journal, 46*(1), 39–50.

Publication manual of the American psychological association. (1994). Washington DC: American Psychological Association.

QSR. (1995). *QSR NUD*IST [Computer Software].* London: Sage.

Raimes, A. (1985). What unskilled writers do as they write: A classroom study of composing. *TESOL Quarterly, 19*, 229–258.

Reid, J. (1992). A computer text analysis of four cohesive devices in English discourse by native and nonnative writers. *Journal of Second Language Writing, 1*(2), 79–108.

Richards, J. C. (Ed.). (1998). *Teaching in action.* Alexandra, VA: TESOL.

Richards, K. (2003). *Qualitative inquiry in TESOL.* New York: Palgrave MacMillan.

Scarcella, R. (1984). How writers orient their readers in expository essays: A comparative study of native and non-native English writers. *TESOL Quarterly, 18*(4), 671–689.

Schegloff, E., Koshik, I., Jacoby, S., & Olsher, D. (2002). Conversation analysis and applied linguistics. *Annual Review of Applied Linguistics, 22,* 3–31.

Schmidt, R. W., & Froda, S. N. (1986). Developing basic conversational ability in a second language: A case study of an adult learner of Portuguese. In R. R. Day (Ed.), *Talking to learn: Conversation in second language acquisition* (pp. 237–326). Rowley, MA: Newbury House.

Silva, T. (1993). Toward an understanding of the distinct nature of L2 writing: The ESL research and its implications. *TESOL Quarterly, 27*(4), 657–677.

Smagorinsky, P. (1994). Think-aloud protocol analysis: Beyond the black box. In P. Smagorinsky (Ed.), *Speaking about writing: Reflections on research methodology.* Thousand Oaks, CA: Sage.

Spada, N., & Fröhlich, M. (1995). *COLT observation scheme.* Sydney: National Centre for English Language Teaching and Research.

Spradley, J. P. (1980). *Participation observation.* New York: Holt, Rinehart & Winston.

Street, B. (1984). *Literacy in theory and practice.* Cambridge, UK: Cambridge University Press.

Swales, J. M. (1990). *Genre analysis.* Cambridge, UK: Cambridge University Press.

Swales, J. M., & Feak, C. (1994). *Academic writing for graduate students.* Ann Arbor: University of Michigan Press.

Swales, J. M., & Feak, C. (2000). *English in today's research world.* Ann Arbor: University of Michigan Press.

Toohey, K. (1998). "Breaking them up, taking them away": ESL students in grade 1. *TESOL Quarterly, 32*(1), 61–84.

Ulichny, P. (1996). Performed conversations in an ESL classroom. *TESOL Quarterly, 30*(4), 739–764.

Upton, T., & Connor, U. (2001). Using computerized corpus analysis to investigate the textlinguistic discourse moves of a genre. *English for Specific Purposes, 20*(4), 313–329.

van Lier, L. (1988). *The classroom and the language learner.* London: Longman.

Wallace, M. (1998). *Action research for language teachers.* Cambridge, UK: Cambridge University Press.

Willett, J. (1995). Becoming first graders in an L2: An ethnographic study of L2 socialization. *TESOL Quarterly, 29*(3), 473–504.

Williams, H. (2004). Lexical frames and reported speech. *ELT Journal, 58*(3), 247–257.

Yin, R. K. (2003). *Case study research design and method.* Thousand Oaks, CA: Sage.

Zamel, V. (1985). Responding to student writing. *TESOL Quarterly, 19*(1), 79–101.

Author Index

Subject Index